Sonn

〜

"Belli was the great master of the dialect and a scholarly recorder of the filth and blasphemy."
Anthony Burgess

"If we think of Belli as the contemporary of the first Romantic generation and the first naturalists, we can assess what an extraordinary phenomenon his poetry is."
Alberto Moravia

"Extraordinary! A great poet in Rome, an original poet... a rare poet."
Sainte-Beuve

"There's so much spice and wit in his poems... and the contemporary life of the Roman people is so realistically portrayed that you cannot help laughing out loud."
Nikolai Gogol

ONEWORLD CLASSICS

Contents

Giuseppe Gioacchino Belli (1791–1863)

A young G.G. Belli

Belli's wife Maria

Belli's son Ciro

Belli's daughter-in-law
Cristina

Belli's friends Francesco Spada (top left) and Amalia Bettini (top right);
the Belli monument in Rome (below)

Belli's autograph corrections to the sonnet
'Il pianto di Pasquino' by Giovanni Giraud

Sonnets

Er ricordo

Er giorno che impiccorno Gammardella
io m'ero propio allora accresimato.
Me pare mó, ch'er zàntolo a mmercato
me pagò un zartapicchio* e 'na sciammella.

Mi' padre pijjò ppoi la carrettella,
ma pprima vorze gode l'impiccato:
e mme tieneva in arto inarberato
discenno: "Va' la forca cuant'è bbella!"

Tutt'a un tempo ar paziente Mastro Titta*
j'appoggiò un carcio in culo, e Ttata a mmene
un schiaffone a la guancia de mandritta.

"Pijja," me disse, "e aricordete bbene
che sta fine medema sce sta scritta
pe mmill'antri che ssò mmejjo de tene."

29th September 1830

The Recollection

The day that Camardella* faced the gallows,
I got confirmed… still seems like yesterday—
Godfather, me, the fairground games I played,
the treats I got (some knick-knacks and marshmallows).

My father booked a two-horse coach for us,
though first there was the hanging to enjoy.
"That scaffold, eh?" he said, "the real McCoy!"
and hoicked me up so I could feel the buzz.

The very moment that the hangman thwacked
the prisoner's sorry arse cheeks into space,
Papa struck a blow across my face—

"Take that," he said, "so one day you'll look back
and understand: this fate is destined to
take down a thousand better men than you."

Er matto da capo (1)

Sai chi ss'è rriammattito? Caccemmetti:
e 'r padrone, c'ha ggià vvisto la terza,
l'ha mmannato da Napoli a la Verza,*
pe rrifajje passà ccerti grilletti.

Lì pprincipiò a sgarrà tutti li letti,
dava er boccio a la dritta e a la riverza:
ma mmó ttiè tutte sciggne pe ttraverza,
e ccià er muro arricciato a cusscinetti.

Che vvòi! Nun t'aricordi, eh Patacchino,
che ggià jje sbalestrava er tricchettracche
sin da quanno fasceva er vitturino?

Che ccasa! Er padre e ddu' fratelli gatti;
la madre cola, e ttre ssorelle vacche:
e ttra ttutti una manica de matti.

3rd October 1831

Mad Again (1)

You know who's flipped again? Loverboy Jack.
His boss – who's seen it all, and knows the score –
has sent him to the Naples nuthouse for
some treatment, so he'll get his marbles back.

But Jack went smashing up the beds, and then
dashing his head against the walls as well,
so now he's in a little padded cell
all strapped and hog-tied like a trussed-up hen.

Ah well! You do remember, don't you lad,
he had a screw loose long ago, for sure,
from when he was a coachman years before.

Christ what a crew! His mum's a grass, his dad's
a crook, his brothers too, and then those sluts
his sisters... Barking mad, the whole lot! Nuts!

Accusì va er monno

Quanto sei bbono a stattene a ppijjà
perché er monno vò ccurre pe l'ingiù:
che tte ne frega a tte? llassel'annà:
tanto che speri? aritirallo su?

Che tte preme la ggente che vvierà,
quanno a bbon conto sei crepato tu?
Oh ttira, fijjo mio, tira a ccampà,
e a ste cazzate nun penzacce ppiù.

Ma ppiù de Ggesucristo che ssudò
'na camiscia de sangue pe vvedé
de sarvà ttutti; eppoi che ne cacciò?

Pe cchi vvò vvive l'anni de Novè
ciò un zegreto sicuro, e tte lo dó:
lo ssciroppetto der dottor Me ne...

14th November 1831

6

The Way of the World

You're much too nice – why put your back out when
the world goes hurtling downhill anyway?
So what's the point? Just let it go, okay—
or do you mean to push it up again?

Who cares about the future – now's enough –
and once you're dead you're dead, that's what I say.
The day to live for, sonny, is today,
don't waste your breath on all this stupid stuff.

Just think of Jesus Christ, who sweated blood
in buckets when he tried to do his bit—
but what the hell did he get out of it?!

To live as long as Noah, and you could,
I've got a surefire secret – you're in luck:
a little cure-all called *Who Gives a...*

Er giorno der giudizzio

Cuattro angioloni co le tromme in bocca
se metteranno uno pe cantone
a ssonà: poi co ttanto de voscione
cominceranno a ddì: ffora a cchi ttocca.

Allora vierà ssu una filastrocca
de schertri da la terra a ppecorone,
pe rripijjà ffigura de perzone,
come purcini attorno de la bbiocca.

E sta bbiocca sarà Ddio bbenedetto,
che ne farà du' parte, bbianca e nnera:
una pe annà in cantina, una sur tetto.

All'urtimo usscirà 'na sonajjera
d'Angioli e, ccome si ss'annassi a lletto,
smorzeranno li lumi, e bbona sera.

25th November 1831

*Judgement Day**

Four portly angels, trumpets raised up high,
will plonk down in the corners at their ease
and blow their horns, and with a booming cry
will start to state their business: "Next up please."

The earth will spew a helter-skelter line
of skeletons on hands and knees, who'll then
assume the bodies of their former times*
and dash about like chicks around a hen.

This hen is not a hen, but God instead,
and He'll divide them into Yes and No:
the Yes will go upstairs, the rest below...

And last, there'll be a big humdinging flight
of angels who, as though it's time for bed,
will blow the candles out, and nighty-night.

Er mortorio de Leone Duodescimosiconno

Jerzera er Papa morto c'è ppassato
propi'avanti, ar cantone de Pasquino.
Tritticanno la testa sur cuscino
pareva un angeletto appennicato.

Vienivano le tromme cor zordino,
poi li tammurri a tammurro scordato:
poi le mule cor letto a bbardacchino
e le chiave e 'r trerregno der papato.

Preti, frati, cannoni de strapazzo,
palafreggneri co le torce accese,
eppoi ste guardie nobbile der cazzo.

Cominciorno a intoccà ttutte le cchiese
appena uscito er morto da palazzo.
Che gran belle funzione a sto paese!

26th November 1831

The Funeral of Pope Leo XII

Last night the late great Pope went cruising by
Pasquino's corner,* right in front of us,
head nodding on a bed of fluffiness
just like an angel kipping on the sly;

and then the muted buglers came on down,
and drummers drumming with a muffled din,
and mules to haul the mighty baldaquin,
and then the papal keys and papal crown;

friars and priests, and next a clapped-out gun,
and grooms who held aloft their flaming tapers,
and then those bloody guardsmen on display.

The bells of all the churches tolled as one
the moment that the corpse went on its way...
This country has such entertaining capers!

La bbona famijja

Mi' nonna a un'or de notte che vviè Ttata
se leva da filà, ppovera vecchia,
attizza un carboncello, sciapparecchia,
e mmaggnamo du' fronne d'inzalata.

Quarche vvorta se fàmo una frittata,
che ssi la metti ar lume sce se specchia
come fussi a ttraverzo d'un'orecchia:
quattro nosce, e la scena è tterminata.

Poi ner mentre ch'io, Tata e Ccrementina
seguitamo un par d'ora de sgoccetto,
lei sparecchia e arissetta la cuscina.

E appena visto er fonno ar bucaletto,
'na pissciatina, 'na sarvereggina
e, in zanta pasce, sce n'annamo a letto.

28th November 1831

The Good Family

My poor old granny leaves her spinning wheel
and pokes the fire when daddy gets back late,
and sets the table for the little meal
we'll sit down to. There's not much on the plate,

perhaps an omelette, cooked so thin and clear
that if you held it up against the sun
you'd see the light shine through it, like an ear;
and then we have some nuts, and then we're done.

While daddy, me and Clemmy take a drop,
granny does some housework here and there,
she needs things spick and span before she'll stop.

It isn't long before the bottle's dead,
and then – a hasty pee, a little prayer –
and thanks to God we take ouselves to bed.

La scirconcisione der Zignore

Sette ggiorni e un po' ppiù ddoppo de cuello
che ccor fieno e li scenci inzino ar gozzo
la Madonna tra un bove e un zomarello
partorì er bon Gesù ppeggio d'un mozzo;

er padre sputativo poverello
pijjò in braccio er bambino cor zangozzo;
e annorno ar tempio a fajje fà a l'uscello
er tajjo d'un tantin de scinicozzo.

Eppoi doppo trent'anni fu pe mmano
de San Giuvanni bbattezzat'a sguazzo
in cuer tevere granne der giordano.

In cuanto a cquesto è vvero ch'er regazzo
venne a la fede e sse fesce cristiano:
ma le ggirelle io nu le stimo un cazzo.

12th January 1832

The Circumcision of the Lord

After the week or so since Mary had
– while chin-deep in a load of rags and hay
between a cow and donkey, where she lay –
borne Jesus, like some lowdown stable lad,

it was the putative and poor old dad
who held Him in his arms and, spirits sinking,
went down the Temple for some plonker-pinking
and had the tiny todger tweaked a tad.

Then after thirty years and by the hand
of John was Jesus Christ baptized – splish-splosh –
in that great Tiber that's the Jordan, and

so all seems fine and dandy, this young man
had found the faith, become a Christian…
But as for turncoats, I don't give a toss.

Li segreti

Ècchete cquà si ccome l'ho ssaputa:
Nanna s'è cconfidata co Vvincenza;
questa l'ha ddetto a Nnina a la Sapienza;*
Nina l'ha ddetto in confidenza a Ttuta.

Ccusì è annato a l'orecchia de Cremenza,
ch'è ccurza a rraccontallo a la bbaffuta:
e llei, ch'è amica mia, oggi è vvienuta
a dimmelo a cquattr'occhi in confidenza.

E s'io l'ho ddetto a tte, sso de raggione
che ttu ssei donna ch'er zegreto mio
l'hai sentito in ziggìr de confessione.

Commare, abbada pe la mórdeddio,
si tte pijjassi mai la tentazzione
de dillo, nu lo dì cche ll'ho ddett'io.

20th January 1832

16

Secrets

Dad-dah! And this is how I came to know:
It's Joannie who confided it to Vic,
who dished the dirt to Nina double-quick,
and Nina clued up May, in private, who

went waggling Clemmie's ears, so Clemmie raced
to tell the bearded lady what she'd found,
and she – a friend of mine – today came round
in confidence to tell me face to face.

And if I've squealed, well that's because I hear
you keep a secret with the same discretion
as priests do in a holy sealed confession...

But mind now – for the love of God, my dear,
if strong temptations kick in, as they do,
don't tell the one you tell that I told you.

Chi va la notte, va a la morte

Come sò lle disgrazzie! Ecco l'istoria:
co cquell'infern'uperto de nottata
me ne tornavo da Testa-spaccata
a ssett'ora indov'abbita Vittoria.

Come llì ppropio dar palazzo Doria
sò ppe ssalì Ssanta Maria 'nviolata,
scivolo, e tte do un cristo de cascata,
e bbatto apparteddietro la momoria.*

Stavo pe tterra a ppiagne a vvita mozza,
quanno c'una carrozza da Signore
me passò accanto a ppasso de bbarrozza.

"Ferma," strillò ar cucchiero un zervitore;
ma un voscino ch'escì da la carrozza
je disse: "Avanti, alò: cchi mmore more."

21st January 1832

Who Travels by Night Is a Dead Man

Well accidents will happen! Here's the score:
that hellish night, I was returning from
Testa-spaccata Street* some time round one—
I'd been to see Victoria before.

I reached Palazzo Doria* and climbed
Santa Maria's* steps, and then kersmack!—
I slipped, I caught my head a dreadful crack
and went down like a deadweight down a mine.

Now as I lay there, whining like a hound,
the carriage of some high-class toff came round
and slow-coached closely past my sad demise.

I heard a bloke on top shout, "Stop a minute!" –
but then there came a sweet voice from within it:
"Drive on, and make it snappy – who dies dies."

Er galantomo

Nun ce vò mmica tanto pe ssapello
si ssei un galantomo o un birbaccione.
Senti messa? sei scritto a le missione?
cuann'è vviggijja magni er tarantello?

a le Madonne je cacci er cappello?
vòi bbene ar Papa? fai le devozzione?
si ttrovi crosce ar muro in d'un portone,
le scompisci o arinfòderi l'uscello?

dichi er zottumprisidio cuanno t'arzi?
tienghi in zaccoccia er zegno der cristiano?
fai mai la scala-santa a ppiedi scarzi?

tienghi l'acquasantiera accapalletto?
Duncue sei galantomo, e ha' tant'in mano
da fà ppuro abbozzà Ddio bbenedetto.

11th November 1832

The Gentleman

It's not exactly difficult or tough
to know if you're a gent or just some hood:
you're keen on Mass and all that mission stuff?*
You stick to fish on Fridays, like you should?

It's hats off to a Lady or a Miss?
You love the Pope? Perform the sacraments?
Those crosses on the walls of tenements,
you keep your todger in or take a piss?*

When getting up, you say a little prayer?
Rosary beads – you've always got some there?
You walk the Scala Santa on your knees?*

There's holy water by your bed at night?
Then you're a gent who's fully bang to rights,
and God can't stop you doing as you please.

La poverella (1)

Benefattore mio, che la Madonna
l'accompaggni e lo scampi d'ogni male,
dia quarche ccosa a una povera donna
co ttre ffijji e 'r marito a lo spedale.

Me lo dà? mme lo dà? ddica: eh rrisponna:
ste crature sò iggnude tal'e cquale
ch'er Bambino la notte de Natale:
dormìmo sott'un banco a la Ritonna.

Anime sante! se movessi un cane
a ppietà! eh, armeno sce se movi lei,
me facci prenne un bocconcin de pane.

Siggnore mio, ma ppropio me lo merito,
sinnò, davero, nu lo seccherei…
Dio lo conzóli e jje ne renni merito.

13th November 1832

22

The Beggarwoman (1)

Please sir, my saviour – ah the Virgin will
be with you in hard times, protecting you –
please spare some coppers for a poor drudge who
has three small children and a husband ill.

Some change sir, spare some change sir? Please let on.
My children here are naked, as you see,
just like the Child at the Nativity.*
Our home's a bench just by the Pantheon.*

Heavens above, this ought to move a hound
to pity us! Well if you're moved by it,
just let me have some bread, a crust or two.

I truly need it sir, one tiny bit,
if not I wouldn't follow you around…
God bless you sir and keep an eye on you.

La quarella d'una regazza

Siggnora sì: la zitella miggnotta
ha ffatto avé ar Vicario er zu' spappiello
quarmente io l'ho infirzata in ner furello
e jj'ho uperto er cancello de la grotta.

Io j'arispose che cquesta è una fotta,
perch'io nun ciò ppiù ppenne in de l'uscello.
E llui mannò er cirusico a vvedello,
e a vvisità ssi llei l'aveva rotta.

"Pe mmé," disse, "neppuro co li guanti
se tocca er mio" – ma cquella porca indeggna
se fesce smaneggià ddietro e ddavanti.

Vanno bbene ste cose? E cchi jj'inzeggna
pe Ccristo, a lloro che ssò ppreti e ssanti,
de discìde sur cazzo e ssu la freggna?

4th December 1832

A Girl's Legal Action

Yes yes, and that unmarried tart, it's true,
has told the vicar stuff along the lines
of how I did her where the sun don't shine,
and breached the portals of her beaver too—

and when I said I couldn't do this act
because I've got no lead inside my pencil,
he sent the doc to poke at my utensil,
and check her pot of honey was intact.

"No way, you won't touch mine—" I told the quack;
"not even wearing gloves." But her, the hussy,
she let herself be prodded front and back.

These priests and saints, what's going on? What makes
them think they're just the job – for pity's sake –
for passing judgements on the cock and pussy?

La madre de le sante

Chi vvò cchiede la monna a Ccaterina,
pe ffasse intenne da la ggente dotta
je toccherebbe a ddì vvurva, vaccina,
e ddà ggiù co la cunna e cco la potta.

Ma nnoantri fijjacci de miggnotta
dìmo scella, patacca, passerina,
fessa, spacco, fissura, bbùscia, grotta,
fregna, fica, sciavatta, chitarrina,

sorca, vaschetta, fodero, frittella,
ciscia, sporta, perucca, varpelosa,
chiàvica, gattarola, finestrella,

fischiarola, quer-fatto, quela-cosa,
urinale, fracoscio, ciumachella,
la-gabbia-der-pipino e la-bbrodosa.

    E ssi vvòi la scimosa,
chi la chiama vergogna e cchi nnatura,
chi cciufèca, tajjola e ssepportura.

6th December 1832

The Mother of Saintly Women＊

Whoever's got a thing for Katie's cunt
should use with very learnèd folk the term
vagina, *vulva*, say, or take a punt
on *Mound of Venus* or on *Cupid's Urn* –

but as for us, us filthy sons of bitches,
it's pussy, beaver, snatch, and tail, and muff,
it's twat, it's frontmost of the dirty ditches,
it's hairy hoop and bearded clam and chuff,

it's cockpit, snapper, front-bum, minge and fanny,
the slit and slot and slat, the beast below,
the love canal, the quim, the nook-and-cranny,

the gash, the thingummy, the so-and-so,
the bacon-butty-fingerpie-poonannie,
the hole, the lucky dip, the dick-depot.

    What really takes the biscuit though,
there's some who say *pudendum*, *nature's bloom*,
and others who say swamp, and trap, and tomb.

Er padre de li santi

Er cazzo se pò ddì rradica, uscello,
ciscio, nerbo, tortóre, pennarolo,
pezzo-de-carne, manico, scetròlo,
asperge, cucuzzòla e stennarello.

Cavicchio, canaletto e cchiavistello,
er giónco, er guercio, er mio, nerchia, pirolo,
attaccapanni, móccolo, bbruggnolo,
inguilla, torciorecchio e mmanganello.

Zeppa e bbatocco, càvola e tturaccio,
e mmaritozzo, e ccannella, e ppipino,
e ssalame, e ssarciccia, e ssanguinaccio.

Poi scafa, canocchiale, arma, bbambino:
poi torzo, crescimmano, catenaccio,
mànnola, e mmi'-fratello-piccinino.

    E tte lascio perzino
ch'er mi' dottore lo chiama cotale,
fallo, asta, verga, e mmembro naturale.

    Cuer vecchio de spezziale
disce Priàpo; e la su' mojje pene –
seggno per Dio che nun je torna bbene.

6th December 1832

The Father of Saintly Men*

For cock you've got the shaft, the horn, the prick,
the trouser snake, the schlong, the happy hammer,
your percy, peter, poker, wonder-whammer,
the bone, the meat-and-veg, the gigglestick,

belly banana, one-eyed python, dick,
the coochie rooter and the sausage slammer,
the wang, the tool, the wham-bam-thank-you-mammer,
the todger, tadger, chopper and the wick,

the beef, your little chap, your Mr Big,
the baby-maker, willy, dirty dangler,
the piece, the prong, the kit, the gear, the rig,

the plunger, dingus, winkle, hairy hanger,
the ding-a-ling, the knob, the jiggy-jig,
the weenie, pecker, dibber and the wanger.

   My doctor knows just what it is,
and tends to call the thing, if I remember,
phallus and *penis*, and the *natural member*;

   the old boy over there calls his
Priapus... should be *painis*, says his wife,
who hasn't had much fun from it in life.

*Er Nibbio**

Viette cqui a ppettinà, pporca, maligna,
perfida, cocciutaccia, profidiosa.
Lo sai cuant'è cche nun ze fa sta cosa?
da st'ottobbre c'annassimo a la vigna.

Che sserve? io strillo, e llei la pidocchiosa
m'arivorta le spalle e sse la ghigna!
Te vòi da vero fà vvienì la tigna,
come si ffussi ggià ppoco tignosa?

Vale ppiù cquer tantin de pulizzìa
che nun zò cche mme dì: ma a ttè ssull'occhi
se tratta che tte viè la porcheria.

T'abbasti de l'affare de li ggnocchi
c'hai fatti jjeri. In de la parte mia
sortanto, sce contai sette pidocchi.

8th December 1832

Scruff-head

Come here and get it combed you filthy swine,
you stubborn, wilful, naughty little sod.
You know how long it's been, do you, you slob?
October, when we went to work the vines.

Oh what's the use – I yell, and look at this,
she turns her nitwit shoulders round to sneer;
already you're a knuckle-head up here,
you can't afford to be a scab-head Miss!

A little personal hygiene is a prize
beyond compare – but look at all this muck,
watch out, or it'll get into your eyes.

And what about the gnocchi that you cooked
for us last night? It wasn't all that great,
I counted seven lice upon my plate.

Er confessore

"Padre…" "Dite il confiteor." "L'ho ddetto."
"L'atto di contrizione?" "Ggià l'ho ffatto."
"Avanti dunque." "Ho ddetto cazzo-matto
a mmi' marito, e jj'ho arzato un grossetto."

"Poi?" "Pe una pila che mme róppe er gatto
je disse for de me: 'Ssi' mmaledetto';
e è ccratura de Ddio!" "C'è altro?" "Tratto
un giuvenotto e cce sò ita a lletto."

"E llì ccosa è ssucesso?" "Un po' de tutto."
"Cioè? Sempre, m'immagino, pel dritto."
"Puro a rriverzo…" "Oh che peccato brutto!

Dunque, in causa di questo giovanotto,
tornate, figlia, cor cuore trafitto,
domani, a casa mia, verso le otto."

11th December 1832

The Confessor

"Father…" "Say the Confiteor."* "I did."
"Contrition?" "Done that too." "Come on, then, quick."
"I shouted at my husband, *Crazy prick!*
and stole some money too, about ten quid."

"And then?" "And then I said, *Damn you you're dead!*
to one of God's own creatures – yes, my cat,
which broke a dish." "There's more, or is that that?"
"There's more. There's this young man. We went to bed."

"What happened there?" "A bit of everything."
"But… always by the front door, can we say?"
"And by the back…" "Oh what an ugly sin!

Now then, because of this young man, this shock,
and with your heart contrite in every way,
come back tomorrow, my place, eight o'clock."

La puttaniscizzia

A mme nun me dì bbene de ste lappe
che vvanno co la scuffia e ccor cappotto*
e mmarceno in pelliccia e mmanicotto,
piene d'orloggi, catenelle e cciappe:

lassamo stà che ppoi nun cianno sotto
mezza camiscia da coprì le chiappe:
tutta sta robba sai da che ccondotto
je viè, Stèfino mio? dar tipp'e ttappe.

Pe la strada gnisuna t'arisponne:
come poi j'ariesce d'anniscosto,
se farìano inzeppà da le colonne.

Ma a nnoi nun ce se venne er zol d'agosto,
perché la casterìa de ste madonne
sta ttutta sana in ner gruggnaccio tosto.

16th December 1832

*Decwhorum**

Don't waste your breath on praising them to me,
these sluts who gad about in furs and muffs
and pretty hats, and strut their fancy stuff
bedecked in watches, chains and jewellery;

let's leave it be that underneath that lot
their bums don't have a stitch of undies on—
you know what pipeline all their clobber's from,
eh Steve? The rumpy-pumpy pipe, that's what.

You wouldn't even get the time of day
from them out here, but in more secret places
they like a big old wham-bam-thank-you-mam.

So we're not fooled by mutton dressed as lamb:
the kind of chastity this lot display
is firmly written in their brazen faces.

L'ingeggno dell'Omo

Er venardì de llà, a la vemmarìa,
io incontranno ar Corzo Margherita,
je curze incontro a bbracciuperte: "Oh Ghita,
propio me n'annerebbe fantasia!"

Disce: "Ma indove?" Allora a l'abborrita
je messe er fongo e la vardrappa mia,
e ddoppo tutt'e ddua in compagnia
c'imbusciassimo drento ar Caravita.

Ggià llì ppare de stà ssempr'in cantina:
e cquer lume che cc'è, ddoppo er rosario
se smorzò pe la santa dissciprina.

Allora noi in d'un confessionario
ce dassimo una bbona ingrufatina
da piede a la stazzione der Zudario.

18th December 1832

The Ingenuity of Man

At evensong on Friday last but one
I met with Margaret in the street outside,
went running up the Corso* arms held wide:
"I'm gagging for it Mags, let's get it on!"

"But where?" she said, so quick as quick can be
I fixed her with my hat and coat to wear
and both of us skedaddled out of there
and in the Garavita* sneakily.

Inside it's dungeon-dark, and any lights
are dimmed down further for the penance rites,
after the rosary is said aloud.

Well then, in a confessional we set to,
and got all hot and bothered, as you do,
just underneath *The Station of the Shroud.**

Er cassiere

Er riscritto disceva: *Antonio Ulivo*
sino da ggiugno scorzo è ggiubilato.
Dunque io curze a pijjà er cuantitativo,
che ffasceva er currente e ll'arretrato.

Disce: "Indov'è la fede der curato
che ffacci vede che vvoi sete vivo?"
"Oh bbella! e io chi ssò, ssiat'ammazzato,
io che parlo, cammino e ssottoscrivo?"

Guasi m'era vienuta bbizzarria
de ddajje er calamaro in mezz'ar gruggno,
com'attestato de la vita mia.

Nun je stavo davanti a cquer burzuggno?
Pascenza avessi avuto fantasia
d'avé una prova ch'ero vivo a ggiugno.

9th January 1833

The Clerk

Anthony Green – the document was clear –
your pension is backdated to last June.
Wahey, I went to get my dosh as soon
as anything, the dues and the arrears.

He says, "And where's your priest's certificate,
to prove that you're alive, and back your claim?"
"Come on!... I walk and talk and sign my name –
I'm me all right, you can be sure of that!"

I almost had the urge to take my fist
and smash his sodding inkwell in his mush,
to see if that would prove that I exist.

Wasn't I right in front of that buffoon?!
I could have understood it if he'd pushed
for proof of my existence back in June...

Er carzolaro ar caffè (1)

Cos'è, ccorpo de Ddio, sor caffettiere,
c'ancóra nun me date sti grostini?
Volete véde c'agguanto un bicchiere
e vve lo fo vvolà ssu li dentini?

Ma vvarda sti fijjacci d'assassini
si cche bber modo d'abbadà ar mestiere!
Io viengo cqui a ppagà li mi' quadrini,
e vvojj'èsse servito de dovere.

Sicuro, sor cazzèo, che ddico bbene:
sicuro, sor mustaccio de falloppa,
che mme se scalla er zangue in de le vene.

Cuann'uno spenne, una parola è ttroppa;
duncue mosca, per Cristo, e ppoche sscene,
o vve faccio iggnottì sta sottocoppa.

13th January 1833

The Cobbler in the Coffeehouse (1)

Hey waiter, what's the deal here, it's a pisser,
how come you haven't brought my rarebit yet?
You think I wouldn't grab a glass, no sweat,
and smash it in your pretty little kisser?

Just look at them, those sons of bitches there,
the way they do their jobs and mess about!
It's my spondulicks here I'm forking out,
they have to treat me right, it's only fair.

Damn right I'm right you low-down shit-for-brains,
damn right my blood is boiling in my veins
you wimpy scraggly-bearded little scrote.

When dishing dosh, one word should do the job,
so put a sock in it and shut your gob,
unless you want this saucer down your throat.

La vita dell'omo

Nove mesi a la puzza: poi in fassciola
tra sbasciucchi, lattime e llagrimoni:
poi p'er laccio, in ner crino, e in vesticciola,
cor tórcolo e l'imbraghe pe ccarzoni.

Poi comincia er tormento de la scola,
l'abbeccé, le frustate, li ggeloni,
la rosalìa, la cacca a la ssediola,
e un po' de scarlattina e vvormijjoni.

Poi viè ll'arte, er diggiuno, la fatica,
la piggione, le carcere, er governo,
lo spedale, li debbiti, la fica,

er zol d'istate, la neve d'inverno...
E pper urtimo, Iddio sce bbenedica,
viè la Morte, e ffinissce co l'inferno.

18th January 1833

*The Life of Man**

Nine months in a bog, then swaddling clothes
and sloppy kisses, rashes, big round tears,
a baby harness, baby walker, bows,
short trousers and a cap for several years,

and then begin the agonies of school,
the ABC, the pox, the six of the best,
the poo-poo in the pants, the ridicule,
the chilblains, measles, fevers on the chest;

then work arrives, the daily slog, the rent,
the fasts, the stretch inside, the government,
the hospitals, the debts to pay, the fucks...

The chaser to it all, on God's say-so,
(after summer's sun and winter's snow)
is death, and after death comes hell – life sucks.

La scrupolosa

Inzomma, cazzo, se pò avé sto bbascio?
se pò ttastà un tantino er pettabbotto?
Ma nnun avé ppavura, che ffo adascio:
cuanto che ssento che cce tienghi sotto.

Ciai scrupolo? e dde cosa? E cche! tte fotto?!
Semo parenti? Sì, ppe vvia der cascio:
cuggini de cuggini: cascio cotto:
parenti come Ggnacchera e ssan Biascio.

Parenti, ggià! cche scrupoli der tarlo!
Per un bascio co mme ttanta cusscenza,
eppoi te fai fischià ddar Padre Carlo.

Ma cche ccredi? che Cristo abbi pascenza
d'abbadà ssi tte bbascio, o ssi tte parlo?
A ste cojjonerie manco sce penza.

22nd January 1833

44

Girl with Scruples

Oh bloody hell, so not one kiss from you?
One little squeeze inside that bra you wear?
Don't worry, I'll be careful what I do,
I only want to feel what's under there…

You've scruples? And for what? We're family and
I might go fucking you?!… Yeah right, oh please—
we're cousins' cousins, can't you understand?
If we're related, so are chalk and cheese!

Related!… God, what namby-pambiness,
and all this bother for a kiss with you
when Father Charles, oh him, he gets a screw!

What's up, you think that Jesus could care less
if you get chatted up by me and kissed?
He doesn't even think of stuff like this.

Er caffettiere fisolofo

L'ommini de sto monno sò ll'istesso
che vvaghi de caffè nner mascinino:
c'uno prima, uno doppo, e un antro appresso,
tutti cuanti però vvanno a un distino.

Spesso muteno sito, e ccaccia spesso
er vago grosso er vago piccinino,
e ss'incarzeno tutti in zu l'ingresso
der ferro che li sfraggne in porverino.

E ll'ommini accusì vviveno ar monno
misticati pe mmano de la sorte,
che sse li ggira tutti in tonno in tonno;

e mmovennose oggnuno, o ppiano o fforte,
senza capillo mai caleno a ffonno
pe ccascà nne la gola de la Morte.

22nd January 1833

The Philosophic Café Proprietor

The people of this world are much the same
as coffee beans inside the grinder's mill:
one's first, one's later and one's later still,
but all are going down towards one doom.

They often chop and change, the bigger beans
jostling the smaller ones and jockeying,
they cram themselves against the metal thing
that crushes all of them to smithereens.

And that's how people live within this world,
all mixed together by a fateful hand
that turns them over – round and round they swirl –

and as they're turning, whether slow or fast,
they sink towards the bottom clueless and
go tumbling down the throat of death at last.

L'allèvo

La mammana protenne che la pupa
me sta ssempre accusì strana e ffurastica,
perché la zinna mia è ttroppa cupa,
e 'r mi' calo è una spesce de scolastica.

Cuant'ar tiro, eh cche vvòi! pare una lupa:
s'attacca ar caporello e mme lo mastica,
e jje dà nnotte e ggiorno, e mme lo ssciupa,
che mme scià ffatto ggià ppiù dd'una crastica.

Oh vvadino mó a ddì: *chi ha mmojje ha ddojje!*
Nun zò ssi cce pozz'èsse paragone
si ppeni più er marito che la mojje.

Vienghino cqui a ssentì er farzo-sbordone
ch'io canto cuanno er petto me s'accojje,
e ddìchino chi ha ttorto e cchi ha rraggione.

11th February 1833

48

Nursing

According to the midwife yesterday,
my little girl is such a savage gripe
because my breasts are wrong – too round, wrong type –
and then the milk inside is more like whey.

What suction, like a wolf! What can I do?
All day and night she's at it on my tit,
chewing the nipple as she tugs on it—
the cracks I've got down there would frighten you.

You know what people say: a *wife means strife*;
But how can they suppose the marriage state
could give the husband more grief than the wife?

Just let them hear the caterwauling song
I'm singing when my nipples suppurate,
and then they'll know who's got it right or wrong.

Er cane

Er cane? a mme cchi mm'ammazzassi er cane
è mmejjo che mm'ammazzi mi' fratello.
E tte dico c'un cane com'e cquello
nun l'aritrovi a ssòno de campane.

Bbisoggna véde come maggna er pane:
bbisoggna véde come, poverello,
me va a ttrovà la scatola e 'r cappello,
e ffa cquer che noi fàmo co le mane.

Ciaveressi da èsse quann'io torno:
me sarta addosso com'una sciriola,
e ppare che mme vojji dà er bon giorno.

Lui m'accompaggna le crature a scòla:
lui me va a l'ostaria: lui me va ar forno...
Inzomma, via, j'amanca la parola.

18th October 1833

The Dog

The dog? I'd rather someone killed my brother
than killed this dog of mine – oh yes, it's true.
Search high and low my friend, I'm telling you,
you won't find one like this, he's like no other.

You want to see him eat, he's like a horse!
You want to see the way, the poor old chap,
he ferrets out my baccy and my cap,
and does the stuff that we do, with his paws.

You'd have to be there, when I'm home, to see
the way he leaps up like an eel at me,
as though he wants to say, "So how are you?!"

He takes the kids to school, he goes off to
the bakers and the pub, he gets things done…
Does everything but speak, in fact, this one.

La vita der Papa

Io Papa?! Papa io?! fussi cojjone!
Sai quant'è mmejjo a ffà lo scarpinello?
Io vojjo vive a mmodo mio, fratello,
e nnò a mmodo de tutte le nazzione.

Lèveje a un omo er gusto de l'uscello,
inchiòdeje le chiappe s'un zedione,
mànnelo a spasso sempre in priscissione
e cco le guardie a vvista a lo sportello:

chiùdeje l'osteria, négheje er gioco,
fàllo sempre campà cco la pavura
der barbiere, der medico e dder coco:

è vvita da fà ggola e llusingatte?
Pe mme, inzin che nun vado in zepportura,
maggno un tozzo e arittoppo le sciavatte.

16th November 1833

Life of the Pope

Me as the Pope?! The Pope?! You're joking, damnit!
I'm better as a cobbler, can't you see?
I want to live in my way, pal, for me,
and not for half the nations on the planet.

To take a fellow's pencil lead away,
to nail him by the arse cheeks to a throne,
to only let him step outside his home
with bodyguards on some procession day...

To have it so he always lives in dread
of barbers, chefs and quacks, to bar him from
the bookie's flutters and the boozer's booze...

is that a life to tempt you? It's a con!
As long as I'm alive instead of dead
I'm okay eating scraps and patching shoes.

Li chìrichi

Li chìrichi de Roma? crosc'e spine!
Dove te vòi scavà ppeggio gginìa?
Uno ruffiano, uno gatto, uno spia,
uno… inzomma canajja senza fine.

Ggiùcheno a zzecchinetto* in zagrestia:
se scóleno oggni sempre l'ampolline:
vonno bbene a le ggente pasqualine*
e vvénneno er bijjetto a cchissesia.

Cor butteghino de le ssedie, intanto,
àzzichen'oggni donna, o cce ssii tata,
o mmamma, o nnonna, o er cornutello accanto.

Serveno messa ch'è un zocché dde tristo;
e cconnìscheno a ccasa l'inzalata
coll'ojjo de le làmpane de Cristo.

29th November 1833

The Sextons

Those Roman sextons eh? For Heaven's sake,
you won't dredge up a more revolting clan.
They're thugs and sneaks and muggers to a man,
an endless load of toerags on the make.

They sit inside the vestry playing poker,
and always polish off the altar wine;
they're fond of church-shy folk at Eastertime,
cos then they get to act as ticket broker,*

and with the profits from their seating scam
they press themselves on every girl they can,
though mum, dad, gran or hubby might be there.

The Mass they put on is a sad affair;
they tap Christ's lamp for oil, and take it home,
and dress their salad with it all alone.

Er madrimonio sicuro

Tu nun capisco indov'abbi la testa.
Hai tanta fernesia de fatte sposa,
e nun zai che cqui a Rroma nun c'è ccosa
che ssii cosa più ffascile de questa.

Vòi marito? E tu àrzete la vesta,
pijjete in corpo una zeppa-bbrodosa,
eppoi va' ddar Curato, e ddijje, Rosa:
"Padre, ajjutate una zitella onesta."

Er prete te dirà: "Cche ccos'è stato?"
Tu allora piaggne, e ddijje: "Un traditore
de l'innoscenza mia m'ha ingravidato."

E cqui accusa qualunque che tte cricca;
ma abbada, pe rriusscìnne con onore,
d'accusà ssempre una perzona ricca.

14th January 1834

A Sure Way to Wed

You must have lost your marbles, one or two:
there's half a dozen ways of getting wed,
and don't you know that here in Rome it's said
that nothing could be easier to do?

You want a husband? Easy, lift your dress,
and clamp a fella's sausage in your thighs,
then find a priest and make your biggest eyes:
"Oh Father, help a maiden in distress!"

The priest will say, "What happened to you, child?"
So blub a bit, then blurt, "I've been defiled!
The fleabag knocked me up then took a hike!"

And then accuse whatever man you like,
but mind – to pull it off with real panache,
accuse a man who isn't short of cash.

*Er testamento der pasqualino**

Torzetto l'ortolano a li Serpenti*
prometteva oggni sempre ar zu' curato
c'a la su' morte j'averìa lassato
cinquanta scudi e ccert'antri ingredienti.

Quanto, un ber giorno, lui casc'ammalato
e ccurreveno ggià cquinisci o vventi
tra pparenti e pparenti de parenti
a mmostrajje un amore indemoniato.

Ècchete che sse venne all'ojjo santo;
e 'r curato je disse in ne l'ontallo:
"Ricordàteve, fijjo, de quer tanto…"

Torzetto allora uprì ddu' lanternoni,
e jj'arispose vispo com'un gallo:
"Oggne oggne, e nnu mme roppe li cojjoni."

6th April 1834

Last Words of a Church-shy Chap

The grocer Mr Corr on Serpent Street
was always making pledges to the priest
that when he croaked he'd leave him, at the least,
a bit of this and that and fifty sheets.

The day that he fell sick, the relatives
and relatives of relatives came knocking,
till fifteen, twenty-odd of them were flocking
with all the passion that true grieving gives.

The holy oil was brought out hurriedly,
and as the priest anointed him he said,
"My son, about that stuff you promised me—"

Corr's eyes flipped open, lanterns in his head,
and lively as a rooster he let rip:
"Just grease me up, okay, and button your lip!"

Er dottore somaro

Corpa sua. E pperché llui nun ze spiega?
Pe cche rraggione l'antra sittimana
rispose ar mi' discorzo in lingu'indiana
quanno me venne a vvisità in bottega?

Dico: "Diteme un po', ssor dottor Bréga,
pò ffà mmale er cenà, cco la terzana?"
Disce: "Abbasta sii robba tutta sana,
tu ppòi puro scenà; cchi tte lo nega?"

Me maggnai dunque sano un paggnottone
casareccio, un zalame, 'na gallina,
'na casciotta, un cocommero e un melone.

Lui, cazzo, aveva da parlà itajjano,
e rrisponneme a mme cquela matina:
maggna robba inzalubbra, e vvàcce piano.

15th April 1834

The Dumb Doctor

His fault – he don't explain himself, you see.
It all took place last week, and inasmuch
as he goes rattling off in Double-Dutch
when coming down my shop to check on me.

"Now Doc, this fever what I've got," I went;
"it means I have to watch out what I scoff?"
He goes, "One's fine when eating wholesome stuff,
my man – one has to eat, mm? Excellent!"

So I eats, whole, some stuff, just like he said:
whole canteloup, whole cheese, whole loaf of bread,
salami, water melon and a hen…

Sod it, he should've spoken proper when
he came that day to bandy words about:
"Scoff top-notch tucker pal, but don't pig out."

Se more

Nun zapete chi è mmorto stammatina?
È mmorto Repisscitto,* er mi' somaro.
Povera bbestia, ch'era tanto caro
da potecce annà in groppa una reggina.

L'ariportavo via dar mulinaro
co ttre sacchi-da-rubbio de farina,
e ggià mm'aveva fatte una diescina
de cascate, perch'era scipollaro.

J'avevo detto: nun me fa la sesta;
ma llui la vorze fà, pporco futtuto;
e io je diede una stangata in testa.

Lui fesce allora come uno stranuto,
stirò le scianche e tterminò la festa.
Poverello! m'è ppropio dispiasciuto.

20th April 1834

Dying

You know who breathed his last as of today?
My donkey, Neddy Knucklehead, has died.
Poor beast, so sweetly natured in his way,
he could have taken royals for a ride.

We'd hardly left the mill a mile or so
with just a small two-hundredweight of load
before he fell, and ten times in a row,
because he kept on stumbling in the road.

I told him straight, *now don't do that again,*
but ah… the fucker did just what he pleased,
and so I punched his lights out there and then.

He gave a little, kind of, sort of, sneeze,
his legs went rigid, and his life kaputted.
Poor fellow, I was absolutely gutted.

L'udienza de li du' Scozzesi

O ssiino du' Scozzesi, o ddu' Scozzoni,
in tutte le maggnère èssi contento
ch'è un gran piccolo seggno de talento
quer méttese a ggirà ssenza carzoni.

Dunque ar paese de sti du' porconi
bbisoggna dì cche nun ce tiri vento;
perché, ssi cce tirassi, oggni momento
j'annerebbeno in mostra li cojjoni.

E un Papa che cconossce le creanze
s'è ppotuto arisorve a ddà l'udienza
a sta sorte de manichi-de-panze?

A rrìsico, per Dio, ch'in zu' presenza,
ne l'inchinasse o in antre scircostanze,
j'avessino da fà cquarche schifenza!

25th April 1834

An Audience with Two Scotsmen*

Scotsmen or coachmen, pal, or anyone—
no matter what they are it makes no odds,
they're nothing but a pair of tasteless sods
to swan around without their trousers on.

Whatever place they're from, the dirty pigs,
you'd have to say there can't be breezes in it,
for just one puff of wind and any minute
they'd end up showing off their Mr Bigs.

To think the Pope, who knows his Ps and Qs,
could go and grant a papal audience
to men like these two good-for-nothing Jocks,

and risk, within his presence, such to-dos!
When bowing low, or some such circumstance,
they might have followed through with aftershocks...

Li dannati

Fijji, a ccasa der diavolo se vede,
tutt'in un mucchio, facce, culi e ppanze,
e ggnisuno llaggiù ppò stacce a sséde
co le duvute e ddebbite distanze.

Figuràteve mó ccosa succede
fra cquelle ggente llà ssenza creanze!
carci, spinte, cazzotti: e ss'ha da crede
scànnoli d'oggni sorte e ggravidanze.

Sì, ggravidanze: e cchi ppò ddì er contrario?
quanno se sa cc'ar giorno der giudizzio
ce s'annerà cco ttutto er nescessario?

Ommini e ddonne! oh ddio che ppriscipizzio!
Come a l'inferno er Cardinal Vicario
troverà mmodo da levajje er vizzio?

29th April 1834

The Damned

My children, in the devil's house one sees
faces and bums and bellies in a heap,
they're packed in like sardines or penned-up sheep
without an inch of space to sit at ease.

Now then, imagine what takes place with these
damned folk, who lack all common decency:
there's kicks and punches and – believe you me –
shockers of every sort, like pregnancies!

Yes pregnancies – what else is there to say,
knowing that on the fateful Judgement Day
you're taken with your little box of tricks?*

Oh God! Disaster! Men and women mixed!
And how's the Vicar General* going to
release them from the vices that they do?

La mi' nora

Mi' fijjo, sì, cquel'animaccia fessa
che ffu pposcritto e annò a la grann'armata,
è ttornato uffizziale e ha rriportata,
azzecca un po'! una mojje dottoressa.

Si ttu la senti! "È un libbro ch'interressa…
Ggira la terra… La luna è abbitata…
Ir tale ha scritto un'opera stampata…
La tal'antra è una bbrava povetessa…"

Fuss'omo, bbuggiarà! mma una ssciacquetta
ha da vienicce a smove li sbavijji
a ffuria de libbracci e pparoloni!

Fili, fili: lavori la carzetta:
abbadi a ccasa sua: facci li fijji,
l'allatti, e nun ce scocci li cojjoni.

12th June 1834

My Daughter-in-Law

My son – oh yes that bad sort, that lowlife
who got conscripted and who served his whack –
is now an officer and has come back
with – take a guess! – an educated wife.

To hear her banging on! "…ab*sorb*ing text…
…those lunar denizens… …the earth's rotation…
…that fellow penned a *splen*did publication…
…the lady is a *marv*ellous poetess…"

For pity's sake! In men it's bad enough,
but being saddled with this chatterbox
and all her lousy books and fancy guff…

She should be spinning wool, and darning socks,
and keeping house, and popping babies out,
and feeding them – not jerking us about!

La lottaria nova (1)

'Ggni ggiorno, accetto er venardì, ar palazzo
de la casa Teòdoli, un'arpia
de chincajjere* fa una lottaria
co una rota che svòrtica un regazzo.

Li bijjetti appremiati hanno un spegazzo
cor nummero der premio che sse pìa.
L'antri sc'è scritto *Alegri*. Alegri un cazzo!
Sce ne fregamo assai de st'alegria.

Bell'alegria d'entrà cco ddu' lustrini,
tirà ddu' bbijjettacci e ttornà ffòra
co le fischiate in cammio de quadrini.

Eppoi che ppremi sò cquanno c'hai vinto?
Figurete c'un prete tirò un'ora,
e abbuscò ddu' speroni e un culo finto.

15th June 1834

This New Lotto Business (1)

Palace Teodoli* is where that mean
old knick-knack seller does his Lotto thing
on every day but Friday, featuring
some kid with a tombola-style routine.

They roughly scrawl on every winning ticket
the numbers of the prizes to be won;
the others say, "Cheer up!" Cheer up my bum!
Hmph, they can take their cheerfulness and stick it!

It's cheerful, sure, to take a fiver in
and buy five tickets – then woosh, it's out you come
with bugger-all to show for what you've done.

And what about the prizes if you win?
A priest I know, who spent a load of cash,
won spurs and padding for a lady's ass.

Zia

Che sse vojjino bbene, che da un mese
lui se la porti a spasso oggni matina,
che vvadino a ffà cquarche scappatina
pe li macchiozzi de Villa Bborghese,

sin qui cce sto: mma cche sse siino prese
scert'antre libbertà, nnun me cammina.
Questo, credete scerto, sora Nina,
sò ttutte sciarle e invidie der paese.

Pe llui, ppò ddarzi che jje l'abbi chiesta:
ciaverà fforze pròvo: nun zaprei:
ma in quant'a mmi' nipote, è ttroppa onesta.

E cche llui né ttant'antri sciscisbei
j'abbino mai potuto arzà la vesta,
questo è ssicuro, e mme l'ha ddetto lei.

18th June 1834

Auntie

That they've been smitten for a month or more,
That every day he squires her round the town,
that now and then they pop out to explore
Villa Borghese's shrubbery and grounds,

I won't deny – but as for claims that they
are up to you-know-what, it isn't true—
Try and believe me, Nina, when I say
it's tittle-tattling gossip through and through.

Now as for him, he might have had a go
and tried it on with her – I wouldn't know –
but not my niece, no chance, she's way too good;

not he nor any other chancer could
slip in her pants and nick her maidenhood—
and that's for sure, because she told me so.

Un ber gusto romano

Tutta la nostra gran zodisfazzione
de noantri quann'èrimo regazzi
era a le case nove e a li palazzi
de sporcajje li muri cor carbone.

Cqua ddiseggnàmio o zziffere o ppupazzi,
o er nodo de Cordiano e Ssalamone:
llà nnummeri e ggiucate d'astrazzione,
o pparolacce, o ffiche uperte e ccazzi.

Oppuro co un bastone, o un zasso, o un chiodo,
fàmio a l'arricciatura quarche sseggno,
fonno in maggnèra c'arrivassi ar zodo.

Quelle sò bbell'età, pper Dio de leggno!
Sibbè cc'adesso puro me la godo,
e ssi cc'è mmuro bbianco io je lo sfreggno.

22nd June 1834

A Very Roman Pastime

The treat that us lot liked the most when small,
the biggest thrill, the real McCoy, the biz,
was finding new-built homes and palaces
and using lumps of coal to trash the walls.

So here we'd doodle numbers, little sums,
and Gordon knots and those of Sollymom,*
and there some Lotto stuff; and then move on
to filthy words and pricks and twats and bums.

Or else we'd take a stone or nail or stick
to gouge the plaster out, and draw a pic
so deep we'd hit the bricks and stuff below.

Those were the days all right, my God. Although,
that said, I like to dabble still, it's true…
and when I see a nice white wall, I do.

L'impinitente

Confessamme! e de che? per che ppeccato?
perché ho spidito all'infernaccio un conte?
perché ho vvorzuto scancellà l'impronte
de l'onor de mi' fijja svergoggnato?

Bbe', una vorta che mm'hanno condannato
nun je rest'antro che pportamme a Pponte.
È mmejjo de morì ddecapitato
che avé la testa co una macchia in fronte.

Ma ssi ddoppo er morì cc'è un antro monno,
no, sti ggiudisci infami e sto governo
nun dormiranno ppiù ttranquillo un zonno;

perché oggni notte che jje lassi Iddio
je verrò avanti co la testa in mano
a cchièdeje raggion der zangue mio.

10th November 1834

*The Unrepentant**

Confess my sins?! What sins? Confess for what?
Because I sent the Count to Hellfire's flames?
Because I wanted to remove the stain
that shamed my daughter's honour like a blot?

So what! Let them condemn me all the same
and take me to the Bridge* without delay;
better to lose my head, and straight away,
than keep it when the forehead's stamped with shame.

If there's a world beyond my death somewhere,
oh, then the judges and the high-up men
will never pass a peaceful night again;

each night that God may grant them, I'll be there—
head in my hands, before them I'll be stood,
to charge them with the spilling of my blood.

Un zentimento mio

Voi dateme una donna, fratèr caro,
che nun abbi un pannuccio, un sciugatore,
un fazzoletto, un piatto, un pisciatore,
una forchetta, un cortello, un cucchiaro.

Voi dàtemela iggnuda e ssenza un paro
de scarpe, o una scopetta, o un spicciatore,
in d'un paese che nun c'è un zartore,
un spazzino, un mercante, o un carzolaro.

Fàtela senza casa e ssenza tetto:
fate de ppiù cche nun conoschi foco,
e nnun zappi che ssia ssedia né lletto.

Figuràteve mó tutta la zella
c'ha d'avé sta donnetta in oggni loco,
eppo' annateme a ddì cch'Eva era bbella.

28th November 1834

My Opinion

And so you give a woman to me, mate,
without a knife and fork, a spoon, a cup,
a handkerchief, a chamberpot, a plate,
a dishcloth and a towel for drying up;

you give her to me nude, without a pair
of shoes, a comb, one sock – and furthermore
you get her from the sticks, from some place where
they lack a tailor's, cobbler's, general store;

and ignorant of fire you give her to me,
of living with a roof above her head,
of knowing what's a chair and what's a bed…

Now picture, if you will, the filth, the muck,
this two-bit woman's caked in – every nook –
then send for me and tell me Eve's a beauty.

Er frutto de la predica

Letto ch'ebbe er Vangelo, in piede in piede
quer bon Padre Curato tanto dotto
se piantò cco le chiappe sul paliotto
a spiegà li misteri de la fede.

Ce li vortò de sopra e ppoi de sotto:
ciariccontò la cosa come aggnede;
e de bbone raggione sce ne diede
più assai de sei via otto quarantotto.

Riccontò 'na carretta de parabbole,
e cce ne fesce poi la spiegazzione,
come fa er Casamia doppo le gabbole.

Inzomma, da la predica de jjeri,
ggira che tt'ariggira, in concrusione
venissimo a ccapì cche ssò mmisteri.

29th November 1834

The Fruits of the Sermon

So having read the Gospel, there and then
that good and learnèd father plonked his rear
against the altarpiece, and – crystal-clear –
explained the mysteries of faith to men;

oh yes, expounded on them inside out,
and every which way told us what they are,
and gave us explanations, more by far
than hundreds, to address our every doubt.

He cited parables, an awful lot,
and gave interpretations, reams and reams,
just like a *Casamia** for your dreams.

In short, and from this sermon that we got,
to sum it up, to say it how it is,
it seems that mysteries are mysteries.

Le crature

Voi sentite una madre. Ammalappena
la cratura c'ha ffatta ha cquarche ggiorno,
ggià è la prima cratura der contorno,
e ssi jje dite che nun è, vve mena.

Conossce tutti, disce tutto, è ppiena
d'un talento sfonnato, è ffatta ar torno,
va cquasi sola, è ttosta come un corno,
e ttant'antri prodiggi ch'è una sscena.

E sta prodezza poi sarà un scimmiotto,
tonto, mosscio, allupato, piaggnolone,
pien de bbava e llattime e ccaca-sotto.

A le madre, se sa, li strilli e 'r piaggne
je pareno ronnò dde Tordinone.*
Le madre ar monno sò ttutte compaggne.

26th December 1834

Kiddiwinkies

Just listen to a mother talking crap:
the brat she drops has barely hit the ground
before she's bragging he's the best around,
and if you disagree you get a slap.

He knows who's who, his gifts run deep, he's full
of talk, he's right as rain, he stands apart—
he's lovely as a finished work of art
and packed with wonders, is this miracle!

In fact he'll be an ugly little monkey,
a stupid, floppy, whining, greedy critter,
a dribbling stinking scabby nappy-shitter.

To mum, the gruntings of this tit-mad junkie
surpass the sweet songs of a West End name.
The mothers of this world are all the same.

Le dimanne a ttesta per aria

Quanno loro s'incontreno, Bbeatrisce,
tu averessi da stà ddietr'un cantone.
"Oh ccaro sor Natale mio padrone!"
"Umilissimo servo, sor Filisce."

Disce: "Ne prende?" "Grazzie tante," disce.
"Come sta?" "Bbene, e llei?" "Grazzie, bbenone."
Disce: "Come lo tratta sta staggione?"
Disce: "Accusì: mmi fa mmutà ccamisce."

Disce: "E la su' salute?" "Eh, nun c'è mmale.
E la sua?" disce. "Aringrazziam'Iddio."
"E a ccasa?" "Tutti. E a ccasa sua?" "L'uguale."

"Ne godo tanto." "Se figuri io."
"Oh ddunque se conzervi, sor Natale."
"Ciarivediamo, sor Filisce mio."

6th February 1835

This and That

And when they run across each other, Bea,
you ought to find a hiding place nearby.
"Why Nat, my dear old fellow, goodness me!"
"Felix – your humble servant, sir, my my!"

One goes, "Tobacco?" "Thanks," the other goes.
"How's life?" "It's fine, and you?" "I'm fine as well."
One goes, "The weather suits you, I suppose?"
"So-so," the other goes. "I'm hot as hell."

One goes, "And how's your health?" "Ah well, not bad –
and you?" the other goes. "Thank God, I'm fine."
"The family?" "All okay – yours too?" "And mine."

"I'm glad to hear it!" "Well I'm likewise glad!"
"Good good, ah well, you take it easy Nat."
"I'll see you later Felix, nice to chat."

Un'erliquia miracolosa

Questo io lo so cche ttra li pezzi rari
d'erliquie che li Papi hanno provisto
e ttiè in conzeggna Monziggnor Zagristo
coll'utentiche drento all'erliquiari,

sc'è er prepuzzio c'aveva Ggesucristo
coll'antri su' membrucci nescessari,
ch'è un erliquione che ssopra all'artari
pò ccacà in faccia ar mejjo che ss'è vvisto.

E nun zerve de dì, ccaro sor Muzzio,
che cc'è ppiù d'un paese che ss'avvanta
d'avé er tesoro der zanto prepuzzio.

Fede, sor Muzzio mio, fede bbisoggna.
Ebbè? mmagaraddio fussino ottanta?
Je sarà aricressciuto come ll'oggna.

14th April 1835

A Miraculous Relic

This much I know: among the rare sensations
and relics that the Popes have gathered for
the prefect of the Sacristy to store
in holy shrines with the authentications,*

Christ's foreskin – plus his other little bits
and vital members – is the pride and joy;*
as relics go it's just the real McCoy,
and any other relic looks like shit

compared… Now then, my dear good sir, don't say
this holy foreskin also seems to hail
from other countries which lay claim to it;

have faith my man, have faith, a little bit.
There could be eighty foreskins? Fine, okay—
perhaps it grew and grew, like fingernails.

Er diavolo a cquattro

La serva no, nnun j'ha sfassciato un vaso,
je róppe un pissciator de porcellana:
pissciatori che llei n'è ttanta vana
che sse li tiè ccome la rosa ar naso.

Pènzete quela povera cristiana!
Se bbuttò ttra la bbraccia a ddon Gervaso
pe intimà a la padrona er fiero caso;
e llei tratanto se serrò in funtana.

L'abbate principiò: "Ssiggnora Checca,
imbassciator nun porta pena": e ddoppo
j'appoggiò la sassata secca secca.

L'inferno che nun fu! ggessummaria!
Povero prete, pijjò ssu er galoppo
come un gatto frustato e scappò vvia.

30th May 1835

Raising the Devil

The servant didn't break an ornament,
no no, it was a porcelain chamberpot—
but Madam loves those potties such a lot,
she dotes upon them like a rose's scent,

so pity that poor girl! And what to do,
but throw herself at Father George, and plead,
and ask him to defend her awful deed—
and hide herself inside the washroom too.

The Father's line? "Now Madam, please be fair,
ambassadors are blameless…" – and with that,
he spilled the beans, no messing, fair and square.

Christ on a bike, the hell that was let loose!
Poor man, he bolted like a scalded cat,
he took off at a gallop and vamoosed!

La notizzia de telèfrico

Ha ssentito, Eccellenza, a ddon Bennardo
che ggran nova j'ha ddato un uffizziale
che ll'ha intesa da un omo ggiù ar bijjardo,
che ll'ha lletta in ner fojjo der giornale?

Disce ch'er Re de Francia, ar baluardo
der Tempio de le guardie nazzionale,
un certo Monzù Ggiàchemo Ggerardo
j'ha sparàt'una machina infernale.

Le palle hanno ammazzato pe ffurtuna
un zubbisso de popolo innoscente,
e ar Re ppoi, ch'era robba sua, ggnisuna!

Chi è stato còrto in testa, chi in ner core,
chi in ne la panza; e er Re e li fijji ggnente!
Ce se vede la mano der Ziggnore!

14th August 1835

Through the Grapevine

Some splendid news from Father Bernard, sir,
who got it from an army officer
who had it from a chap at billiards
who read it in the paper earlier—

The King of France* was in the *Booliyard
doo Temply** wotsit with the National Guard
when this almighty shooting match occurred,
caused by a certain *Monsure Jack Gerard.**

By great good fortune, though, the missiles hit
a load of people who were innocent,
and not the King for whom the shots were meant;*

heads and chests and bellies blown to bits,
and yet the King and all his children missed!*
Surely we see the hand of God in this!

Madama Lettizzia

Che ffa la madre de quer gran colosso
che ppotava li Re cco la serecchia?
Campa de *cunzumè*, nnun butta un grosso,
disce *uì* e *nnepà*, sputa e sse specchia.

Sta ssopr'a un canapè, ppovera vecchia,
impresciuttita llì ppeggio d'un osso;
e ha ppiù ccarne sto gatto in d'un'orecchia
che ttutta quella che llei porta addosso.

A ccolori è er ritratto d'un cocommero
sano: un stinco je bbatte co un ginocchio;
e ppe' la vita è ddiventata un gnommero.

Cala oggni ggiorno e vva sfumanno a occhio.
Semo all'Ammèn-gesù: ssemo a lo sgommero:
semo all'urtimo conto cor facocchio.

8th September 1835

Madame Letizia*

The mother of that great colossus, he
whose sickle mowed down kings – know what she does?
She sucks on "zoup", and spits, and says "wee wee";
she counts her pennies, lifts her looking glass,

and lies down on her couch, the poor old dear,
as thin as any manky dried-out bone;
my pussy cat's got more meat on one ear
than pads the body of this poor old crone.

Her colour is a watermelon green,
she's got a gammy ankle from a fall,
her stomach's like a tiny scrunched-up ball.

She's shrinking, from what is to what has been…
We're at the last Amen, her ending's start,
here comes the final bill, and the funeral cart.

Li spaventi de la padrona

E jjerzera me diede un'antra stretta.
Doppo accesi li lumi, a un quarto e mmanco,
stavo in zala accusì ssur cassabbanco
sbavijjanno e bbattenno la scianchetta,

quanno, che vvòi sentì!, de punt'in bianco
quela testa de matta mmaledetta
me se mette a strillà da la toletta
c'uno scorpione je sbramava un fianco.

Curro de furia, spalanco la porta,
e ttrovo lei che sse vieniva meno
sopr'a la cammeriera mezza morta.

Credi che ffussi uno scorpione? Eh ggiusto!
Era un pizzo d'un osso-de-bbaleno,
che jj'ussciva cqui ggiù ffora der busto.

8th September 1835

M'Lady's Panics

Last night she made me have another fit.
I'd lit the lamps against the evening gloom
and sat me down inside the drawing room,
feet tapping as I tried to rest a bit,

when – Jesus Christ – I jumped out of my skin
as suddenly I heard that crazy bat
go screaming murder from her toilet that
a scorpion was trying to do her in.

I ran like hell, went bursting through the door,
and found her passing out and almost prone
across a half-dead maid whose wits had gone.

You really think it was a scorpion?
Yeah right, and not the piece of whale bone
which stuck out of the corset that she wore.

La primaròla

E accusì? ggrazziaddio, sora Susanna,
l'avemo arzata poi la trippettona?
Che la bbeata Vergine e Ssant'Anna
ve protegghino, e ssia coll'ora bbona.

E in che lluna mó state? Ah, in de la nona.
Eh, ar véde, si la panza nun inganna,
pare che nun dev'èsse una pissciona,
ma ssarà arfine quer ch'Iddio ve manna.

Ve la sentite in corpo la cratura?
Dunque bboni bbocconi, e ccamminate;
e llassate fà er resto a la natura.

Ggnente: tutte ssciocchezze. Voi penzate,
pe llevàvve da torno la pavura
quante prima de voi sce sò ppassate.

15th September 1835

The Pregnant Mum

No kidding? Well praise be to God, Susanna,
you're really well and truly up the duff!
I hope the Holy Virgin and Saint Anna
protect you now – and when you do your stuff.

What month are you? Mm-hm, the ninth you say?
If bellies tell the truth, to look at it
it's not a girl, the bundle on its way,
though in the end you'll get what God deems fit.

And can you feel him kick, the little man?
Then walk a bit, get plenty food and drink,
and leave the rest to nature's ancient law…

None of your nonsense, now, come on, just think
– to chase away the terrors, if you can –
how many have been through all this before.

Er traccheggio

"Ebbè? cquanno te sbrighi?" "A ffà cche ccosa?"
"A sposamme." "A sposatte?!" "Sì, a sposamme."
"Sorella, dàmme un po' de tempo, dàmme:
tu ssei 'na donna troppa pressciolosa."

"Sì, ttempo e ttempo, e nun viè mmai." "Ma, Rrosa,
vò ddì cch'averà mmale in ne le gamme."
"E intanto mamma bbrontola." "Eh, le mamme
nun zann'antro che ddì: mmi' fijja è sposa."

"Dunque sciariparlamo cor Curato;
perch'io, bbrutt'animaccia de ggiudìo,
la carne mia, la carne mia t'ho ddato."

"Ma ssenti co che mmeriti se n'essce!
Tanti sussurri pe sta carne! E io,
bbuggiarona che ssei, t'ho ddato pessce?"

16th September 1835

Buying Time

"When will you get a move on, eh?" "What for?"
"To marry me." "To marry you?!" "That's it."
"But baby, give it time, just wait a bit;
a woman in a rush, that's you for sure."

"Oh yeah, I wait for Time – which never comes!"
"That's Time for you, it drags its heels and tarries."
"And meanwhile mother's grumbling." "Ah these mums,
they've got a one-track mind: '*My daughter's married…*'"

"Well then, you'll soon be hearing from my priest,
cos *I*, you dirty, ugly little beast,
have granted you my flesh – that's right, my flesh!"

"But listen to your fancy guff! Oh yes,
you whinge about this flesh, you whine and bleat—
and didn't *I*, you bitch, slip you my meat?"

Le chiamate dell'appiggionante

"Sora Sabbella." "Èe." "Ssora Sabbella,
affacciàteve un po' ssu la loggetta."
"Èccheme: che vvolete sora Bbetta?"
"Ciavéte una piluccia mezzanella?"

"Ciò cquella de la marva." "Ah, nno, nno cquella."
"Eh, nun ciò antro, fijja bbenedetta."
"Bbe', imprestateme dunque un fil d'erbetta,
un pizzico de spezzie e una padella?"

"Mó vve le calo ggiù ccor canestrino."
"Dite, e mme date uno spicchietto d'ajjo,
un po' d'onto e una lagrima de vino?"

"Ma ffàmose a ccapì, ssora Bbettina,
a ppoc'a ppoco voi, si nun me sbajjo,
me sparecchiate tutta la cuscina."

16th September 1835

Calls from the Tenant

"Hey Isabel, hey Isabel!" "Hey what?"
"Lean out the window will you, I'm down here."
"What *is* it Betty? – here I am my dear."
"I don't suppose you'd have a cooking pot?"

"I've only got a mallow pot."* "Oh damn,
I need a cooking pot." "I've none to share."
"Well would you have some other stuff to spare—
a sprig of parsley, spice, a frying pan?"

"I'll drop them down inside the little basket."*
"And what about – it's okay if I ask it? –
a clove of garlic? Drop of wine? Some lard?"

"I know your game, my girl, it isn't hard
to spot it, no – if I don't kid myself,
you're clearing out my kitchen shelf by shelf."

Er pupo (1)

Che bber ttruttrù! oh Ddio mio che cciammellona!
No, pprima fate servo a nnonno e zzio.
Fàteje servo, via, sciumàco mio,
e ppoi sc'è la bbebbella e la bbobbóna.

Bbravo Pietruccio! E ccome fa er giudìo?
Fa aéo? bbravo Pietruccio! E la misciona?
Fa ggnào? bbravo Pietruccio! E cquanno sona?
Fa ddindì? bbraavo! E mmó, ddove sta Iddìo?

Sta llassù? bbraavo! Ebbè? e la pecorella?
Fate la pecorella a zzio e nnonno,
eppoi sc'è la bbobbóna e la bbebbella.

Oh, zzitto, zzitto, via: nòo, nnu la vonno.
Eccolo er cavalluccio e la sciammella…
Eh, sse stranissce un po', mma è ttutto sonno.

20th September 1835

The Toddler (1)

A pretty horsey! And a cakie-wakie!
No no, first greet your uncle and your gramps.
Go greet them, off you go my little scamp,
and *then* the pretty plaything and the cakie.

Terrific Pete! And what do rag-men say?
A-*hooooy*? Terrific Pete! And cats as well?
Me-*ooow*? Terrific Pete! A clanging bell?
Ding-*dong*? Terrific! Where does Jesus stay?

Up there? Terrific! Now, a little sheep?
Let gramps and uncle see the sheep you do,
and then the cake and pretty wotsit too.

All right, hush hush, enough – they want a break.
Come get your pretty horsey and your cake…
Ah me, he's all worked up, he needs a sleep.

Er pupo (2)

Àjo, commare mia, àjo che ffiacca!
Tenello tutto er zanto ggiorno in braccio!
Mai volé stà in ner crino! mai p'er laccio!
Io nu ne posso ppiù: ssò ppropio stracca.

Lo vedete? Mó adesso me s'attacca
e mme la tira inzin che nun è un straccio.
Uf, che vvita da cani! oh cche ffijjaccio!
Làssela, ciscio, via: fermo, ch'è ccacca.

Bbasta, Pietruccio mio, bbasta la sisa.
Dàjjela un po' de pasce a mmamma tua...
Ecco er pianto. Che ggioia, eh sora Lisa?

Ssì, ssì, mmó jje menàmo ar caporello.
Bbrutta sisaccia, c'ha ffatto la bbua
a li dentìni de Pietruccio bbello.

20th September 1835

The Toddler (2)

Ai-ee, my dear, oh my, I don't feel well!
I've held him in my arms the whole day through!
He hates his stroller and his harness too!
I can't go on like this, I'm shot to hell!

Now watch him, latching on, but what to do?
He'll suck until my tit's a wrung-out rag!
A dog's life, mine! Oh yes, the scalliwag!
No sweetie, don't touch that, it's poopy-poo.

Now that's enough, my Pete, we're down to drops,
so let your mummy have a little breather.
Uh-oh, here comes the blubbing – bliss eh, Lisa?

That's right, my baby, what a naughty teat!
We'll smack it on the botty, darling Pete,
for being mean to baby's cheeky chops.

La famijja poverella

Quiete, crature mie, stàteve quiete:
sì, ffijji, zitti, ché mmommó vviè Ttata.
Oh Vvergine der pianto addolorata,
provedéteme voi che lo potete.

No, vvisscere mie care, nun piaggnete:
nun me fate morì ccusì accorata.
Lui quarche ccosa l'averà abbuscata,
e ppijjeremo er pane, e mmaggnerete.

Si ccapìssivo er bene che vve vojjo!…
Che ddichi, Peppe? nun vòi stà a lo scuro?
Fijjo, com'ho da fà ssi nun c'è ojjo?

E ttu, Llalla, che hai? Povera Lalla,
hai freddo? Ebbè, nnun méttete llì ar muro:
viè in braccio a mmamma tua che tt'ariscalla.

26th September 1835

The Poor Family

Now hush my darlings, hush my little ones,
your daddy's coming soon so don't you worry…
Oh Holy Blessèd Virgin Mother Mary,
you who can help me – help me, just this once.

Flesh of my flesh, don't cry, don't cry my sweet
dear lambs, don't make me die with grief for you.
Your daddy will have scrounged a scrap or two,
and we will get some bread, and you will eat.

If you could understand a mother's love…
What's that, Joey, what are you frightened of?
The dark? But son, I've got no oil to light.

And Laura, what, what is it, little mite?
You're cold? Well then, don't sit there all alone,
come to your mummy's arms and warm your bones.

Cosa fa er Papa?

Cosa fa er Papa? Eh ttrinca, fa la nanna,
taffia, pijja er caffè, sta a la finestra,
se svaria, se scrapiccia, se scapestra,
e ttiè Rroma pe ccammera-locanna.

Lui, nun avenno fijji, nun z'affanna
a ddirigge e accordà bbene l'orchestra;
perché, a la peggio, l'urtima minestra
sarà ssempre de quello che ccommanna.

Lui l'aria, l'acqua, er zole, er vino, er pane,
li crede robba sua: *È tutto mio*;
come a sto monno nun ce fussi un cane.

E cquasi quasi goderìa sto tomo
de restà ssolo, come stava Iddio
avanti de creà ll'angeli e ll'omo.

9th October 1835

What Does He Do, the Pope?

What does he do, the Pope? He fools around,
has sleepy-poos, drinks coffee, stuffs his face,
waves from the window, slobs around the place,
takes Rome to be his private stomping ground.

No brats for him – he couldn't give a toss
about a big supporting band of kids,
since even if the city hits the skids
there'll always be some soup left for the boss.

The water, air and sun, the bread and wine,
he thinks he owns the lot – *it's mine, all mine!* –
as if the whole shebang's a one-man show.

It's like the sly old dog would love to find
himself alone – as God was, years ago,
before He made the angels and mankind.

Le smammate

Dìllo, visscere mie de ste pupille:
di', ccore, chi vvò bbene a Mmamma sua?
Uh ffijjo d'oro! E cquanti sacchi? Dua?
Du' sacchi? E Mmamma sua je ne vò mmille.

No, bbello mio, nu le toccà le spille:
sta' attenta, sciscio, che tte fai la bbua.
Oh ddio sinnóe! Oh ppòvea catùa!
S'è ppuncicato la manina Achille!

Guarda, guarda er tettè, ccocco mio caro...
Bbe', er purcinella sì... Nno er barettone...
Ecco la bbumba, tiè... Vvòi er cucchiaro?

Oh, zzitto llì, cché mmó cchiamo bbarbone,
e vve fo pportà vvia dar carbonaro
che vve metti in ner zacco der carbone.

3rd November 1835

Coochy-coochy-coo

But say it, apple of my flesh and blood—
who loves his mummy by the shed-load? You?
How many shed-loads sweetie? Only two?
Your mummy loves you shed-loads by the flood!

No no, don't touch those pins, my little bear,
be careful not to hurt yourself, sweet pea.
Now – oh my goodness, baby, dearie me,
has Archie pricked his little hand? There there...

Look at the doggy, darling, see, pat pat...
You want the doll? Okay... No, not the hat...
A drinkie, here... Now what? You want the spoon?

Oh hush now, or I'll call the coalman soon,
the bogeyman, to carry you away
and lock you in the coal-shed for the day.

L'Avocato Cola

Ma eh? Cquer povero Avocato Cola!
Da quarche ttempo ggià ss'era ridotto
che ssì e nno aveva la camiscia sotto,
e jje toccava a ggastigà la gola.

Ma ppiuttosto che ddì cquela parola
de *carità*, ppiuttosto che ffà er fiotto,
se venné ttutto in zette mesi o otto,
for de l'onore e dd'una ssedia sola.

Mó un scudo, mó un testone, mó un papetto,
se maggnò, ddisgrazziato!, a ppoc'a ppoco
vestiario, bbiancheria, mobbili e lletto.

E ffinarmente poi, su cquela ssedia,
senza pane, senz'acqua e ssenza foco,
ce serrò ll'occhi e cce morì dd'inedia.

8th November 1835

Nicholas, the Lawyer

Really? The lawyer? Poor old Nicholas!
So down at heel for so long that who knows
if he was wearing pants beneath his clothes,
or how he fended off his hungriness.

But rather than complaining everywhere,
and rather than go pleading charity,
in seven months he sold his property,
the lot – except his honour, and one chair.

A hundred quid for this, and ten for that,
and bit by bit the wretch was looking at
no furniture, no clothes, no sheets, no bed.

So finally he sat down on that seat,
no fire for warmth, no food and drink to eat,
and closed his eyes and starved till he was dead.

Li gatti dell'appiggionante

Ma ddavero davero, eh sora Nina,
nun volemo finìlla co sti gatti?
Jerzera me sfassciòrno quattro piatti:
oggi m'hanno scocciato una terrina.

Uno me te dà addosso a la gallina:
l'antro me sporca li letti arifatti...
E oggnisempre bbisoggna che commatti
a ccaccialli a scopate da'a cuscina.

Ecco, er pupo oggi ha er gruggno sgraffiggnato.
E pperché ho da soffrì ttutti sti guasti?
P'er vostro luscernario spalancato?

Quanno le cose sò ddette una, dua,
tre e cquattro vorte, me pare c'abbasti.
Lei se tienghi li gatti a ccasa sua.

27th February 1837

The Tenant's Cats

Well come on Nina, really, have a heart,
now can't we deal with all these cats at last?
Last night they broke four dishes, for a start;
today it was a salad bowl they smashed;

there's one of them been gunning for my hen,
another's done a whoopsie on my sheets,
and all the time it does my head in when
I have to chase them out into the streets.

And look – they've scratched the baby's kisser, see?
And why do I put up with all this stuff?
Because your window's always open wide!

When something's said not once or twice but three,
four times on top, well surely that's enough—
Missus, keep your sodding cats inside.

Er padrone bbon'anima

È ito in paradiso. Morze jjeri,
povero galantomo, in d'un assarto
d'àsima a ttredisciora men'un quarto
quann'io stavo ssciacquanno li bbicchieri.

Tutto pe ccausa de st'infame apparto
de li letti da dà a li granattieri.
Eh, sposa mia, sò stati li penzieri,
che ffanno peggio de mazzola e squarto.

Nun c'è rrimedio, lui, fin dar momento
che pprincipiò a rrimette de saccoccia
parze un pezzo de lardo a ffoco lento.

S'era arrivato a strugge a ggoccia a ggoccia
che in ne li panni sce bballava drento
come una nosce secca in ne la coccia.

4th March 1837

The Good-hearted Boss

He's gone to heaven – snuffed it yesterday,
the poor old buffer, when a sudden bout
of asthma struck at seven, thereabouts,
while I was rinsing plates as is my way.

I blame this bloody contract that he made,
supplying grenadiers with cut-price beds;
ah wife, the worrying inside our heads
can hurt us more than being hanged and flayed…

It finished him, and from that moment, well,
his debts went through the roof and even higher,
and drip by drip, like lard before the fire,

he disappeared before my very nose
until his body danced inside his clothes,
just like a dried-out nut inside its shell.

Li connimenti

Sì, è bbona la cuscina co lo strutto;
anzi lo strutto er barbiere m'ha ddetto
ch'è un connimento che ffa bbene ar petto
come fa er pepe c'arifresca tutto.

S'addatta a li grostini cor presciutto…
ar pollame… a l'arrosto de lommetto…
a lo stufato… all'ummido… ar guazzetto…
ma addoprallo in ner fritto è un uso bbrutto.

Vòi frigge er pessce co lo strutto?! Eh zzitto.
Er pessce-fritto in nell'ojjo va ccotto:
l'ojjo è la morte sua p'er pessce-fritto.

Che mmaggnà da stroppiati! io ne sò mmatto.
E gguarda er Papa, che davero è jjotto:
ce se lecca li bbaffi com'un gatto.

12th March 1837

The Ingredients

Yeah, when it comes to cooking, lard's the best.
Matter of fact, my barber said it could
do wonders for the health, a power of good,
like pepper – puts some hairs upon your chest!

With bacon it's a dream, with rarebits it's
the business, chicken too, and roasted meat,
and as for stews and sauces, works a treat—
but using it to fry in, that's the pits.

You want to fry your fish in lard? You'll spoil
it, whitebait should be fried in olive oil,
your oilve oil's the stuff for frying fish.

Delicious! Oh I'm nuts about that dish,
and so's the Pope, just look at him, so fat!
He licks it off his whiskers like a cat!

Er tartajjone arrabbiato

Che-cche annàte ssspaargènno ch'ìo me-mméno
sch-schia-sschiàffi e ppuu-ppùggni a Mmà-Mmarìa?
Chi-cchì v'iinfórma si a cca-ccàsa mia
cé-cee-cce-céno o nnu-nnu-nnùn ce-céno?

Co-ccome dìte cch'io rru-rrùbbo er fieno
e bbia-bbiastìmo all'o-ll'o-ll'ooòsterìa?
Fi-ffinìtela un po' dd-e fà ll-a spìa,
o vve bb-ùggero a ccè-cce-ccèl zeréno.

Me-mme spiègo cchia-cchiàro, sooór trommétta?
Abb-abbadàte a li faattàcci vostri,
oo cc'è un ber bba-bbastóne cheé vv'aspetta.

E ddì-ddìtelo pù-puu-ppùro a cquelle
sch-sch-scrofàcce, a cque-cque-cquelli mostri
de le vò-vvo-vvo-vvòo-vvostre sorelle.

23rd November 1843

The Enraged Stutterer

W–why are you s–spreading round the lie
I duff Maria up and t–t–tup her?
And who inf–f–f–forms you whether I
am in or not at night for s–s–supper?

How c–c–come you say I steal the hay,
and shoot my m–m–mouth off when I drink?
If you don't quit b–blabbering away,
I'll sort you out when you l–least th–think.

C–catch my drift, M–Mr Nosy Parker?
Butt out, or else your life will get d–darker,
I'll t–t–t–t–take a stick to you—

and tell those ugly c–c–cows t–too,
those m–m–m–m–monstrous evil twisters,
your s–s–s–s–s–s–s–s–sisters.

Mastr'Andrea vedovo

Ripijjà mmojje tu?! Ddoppo le pene
diliggerite co cquel'antra vacca?!
Dunque la tu' pascenza nun è stracca
de pagà le tu' corna a ppranzi e ccene?

Eppoi, ne l'età ttua, te sta mmó bbene,
cardèo mio bbello, de sposà una stacca?
Sai c'a cquesta je bbruscia la patacca,
e ttu ppoco ppiù ssangue hai ne le vene.

Ggiudizzio, mastr'Andrea: nun curre er risico
d'aribbuttatte in d'un inferno uperto
pe vvive disperato e mmorì ttisico.

Annà a impicciasse co rregazze un boccio!
Zzitto, nun t'inquietà: lo so de scerto
c'hai ggià vvotato er tu' primo cartoccio.

9th December 1844

Andrew, the Widower

Another wife?! And after the to-do
you had to stomach from that other cow?
You mean to say you're not fed up somehow
with funding them to go and cheat on you?

Well then, you really think, you shit-for-brains,
that now's the time to marry some young filly?
Her fanny will be burning for a willy,
and you've got little sap left in your veins.

Judgement, Andrew – let's not take the chance
of plunging straight into that gaping hell
and knackering yourself to death as well.

Old codgers, chasing totty and romance!
For pity's sake! As if I didn't know—
you used up all your ammo years ago.

Li malincontri

M'aricordo quann'ero piccinino
che Ttata me portava for de porta
a rriccojje er grespigno, e cquarche vvorta
a rrinfrescacce co un bicchier de vino.

Bbe', un giorno pe la strada de la Storta,
dov'è cquelo sfassciume d'un casino,
ce trovassimo stesa llì vviscino
tra un orticheto una regazza morta.

Tata, ar vedella llì a ppanza per aria
piena de sangue e cco 'no squarcio in gola,
fesce un strillo e ppijjò ll'erba fumaria.

E io, sibbè ttant'anni sò ppassati,
nun ho ppotuto ppiù ssentì pparola
de ggirà ppe li loghi scampaggnati.

15th April 1846

A Terrible Encounter

My mind goes back to being young again,
when daddy used to take me foraging
for country herbs and leaves, with now and then
a glass of wine before continuing,

when one day, near La Storta, by the road
– stretched out and hidden in a nettle bed
not far from where the ruined farmhouse stood –
we stumbled on a girl, and she was dead.

And when he saw her, belly up and bare
and bloodied tip to toe, her throat slit wide,
my daddy shrieked and ran away from there.

And I, although so many years have gone,
can't bear it even now if anyone
suggests a ramble in the countryside.

Note on the Text

The Romanesco text in the present edition is largely based on *Poesie romanesche*, edited by Roberto Vighi (Rome: Libreria dello Stato, 1988–93, 10 vols.) and *I sonetti*, edited by Giorgio Vigolo (Milan: Mondadori, 1952, 3 vols.), with occasional emendations by the Publisher. Belli's idiosyncratic transliteration of the Romanesco dialect has been preserved throughout. Only a selection of Belli's own textual notes has been reproduced below.

Notes

p. 2, *zartapicchio*: A plaything attached to a length of elastic (BELLI'S NOTE).

p. 2, *Mastro Titta*: The name by which hangmen are known in Rome (BELLI'S NOTE).

p. 3, *Camardella*: Antonio Camardella, who crops up in several of Belli's sonnets, was a murderer executed in 1749. He became a popular legend for his refusal to repent or to accept any kind of religious consolation. A celebrated priest was brought in to persuade him to change his mind, and spent an entire day conjuring up the eternal torments of hell. But Camardella would not be moved and went to his death without having received the sacraments, the last rites, or any of the rituals that the Catholic religion prescribes.

p. 4, *Verza*: The town of Aversa, in the Campania region.

p. 9, *Judgement Day*: Belli has a fondness for taking the grand set pieces of Christian theology – in this case, the Day of Judgement, but see also 'The Circumcision of the Lord', p. 15, and the Adam and Eve poem 'My Opinion', p. 79 – and subverting their grandeur with bathetic language and an almost slapstick narrative.

p. 9, *assume the bodies of their former times*: According to several biblical sources, when the world ends there will be a Day of Judgement in the Vale of Jehoshaphat, just outside

Jerusalem; it was believed that the souls of everyone who has ever lived will be temporarily reunited with their bodies – an idea which is also explored to great comedic effect and theological absurdity in 'The Damned', p. 67.

p. 11, *Pasquino's corner*: Pasquino is Rome's most famous "Statua parlante" or "talking statue", on whose pedestal political satires (the so-called "pasquinate") addressed to the most eminent figures – including popes – were attached overnight. The statue, a mutilated fragment of a Hellenistic sculpture, is located in Piazza Pasquino in Rome.

p. 16, *Sapienza*: A district in Rome.

p. 18, *la momoria*: Memory. The common view was that the memory resided towards the back of the skull, so Belli is using the word *momoria* to refer to the back of the head.

p. 19, *Testa-spaccata Street*: Via di Testa Speccata, a street in Rome that no longer exists due to building work at the end of the nineteenth century.

p. 19, *Palazzo Doria*: A palace on Via del Corso, the main thoroughfare of Rome.

p. 19, *Santa Maria*: The church of Santa Maria in Via Lata.

p. 21, *mission stuff*: During this time missions were set up by the respectable to promote the preaching of sermons in the streets.

p. 21, *Those crosses… piss*: It was the habit of many tenement dwellers in Rome to urinate in the shared courtyards outside – where there was generally a crucifix or two – rather than to use a chamberpot indoors.

p. 21, *You walk the Scala Santa on your knees*: This is a form of devotion still practised today by the faithful, who ascend on their knees the twenty-eight marble steps of the Scala Santa – the Holy Staircase that Christ is said to have walked up when he was tried before Pontius Pilate. The staircase was reputedly brought to Rome by St Helena *c.*326 AD, and is today housed in the the Chapel of San Lorenzo, also known as the Sancta Sanctorum, near the Lateran.

p. 23, *the Nativity*: This is perhaps a reference not just to the actual Nativity, but to the Christmas crib erected every year outside St Peter's.

p. 23, *Our home's... Pantheon*: This bench is for sleeping under; Belli's note to the original tells us that chicken vendors used the benches by day for selling their wares. The Pantheon is popularly known as "La Ritonna" (in Italian "La Rotonda").

p. 27, *The Mother of Saintly Women*: With the title of this poem, and that of the partner poem on p. 29, 'The Father of Saintly Men', Belli is pointing out that the body – via the vagina and the penis – physically generates even the highest spiritual achievers. But one suspects his primary aim in these poems is merely to put on a virtuoso display of vulgarity.

p. 29, *The Father of Saintly Men*: See the note above.

p. 30, *Er Nibbio*: A name given to someone with unkempt, dirty hair (BELLI'S NOTE). It literally means "The hawk".

p. 33, *Confiteor*: A prayer of public confession.

p. 34, *cappotto*: A feminine style of headwear (BELLI'S NOTE).

p. 35, *Decwhorum*: Belli's Romanesco title 'La puttaniscizzia' is a mangling of "pudicizia" ("modesty") with "puttana" ("whore"), hence the English title from *decorum* and *whore*.

p. 37, *the Corso*: Via del Corso, see note to p. 19.

p. 37, *the Garavita*: The Church of St Ignatius of Loyola, founded by Father Caravita of Terni. It had a particular renown as a place of piety, and so represents a singularly inappropriate venue for the assignation described in the poem.

p. 37, *The Station of the Shroud*: A depiction of Christ's entombment. It is the last of the fourteen *Stations of the Cross*, a series of paintings or carvings seen around the walls of many churches, in which Christ's final journey is traced from Pilate's house to Calvary and then to his tomb. The faithful used to visit such images in order, as a form of devotion.

p. 43, *The Life of Man*: This sonnet, with its desolate depiction of man's life, is widely regarded as one of Belli's masterpieces.

p. 54, *zzecchinetto:* A card game similar to faro (BELLI'S NOTE).

p. 54, *ggente pasqualine*: People who receive Holy Communion and go to church only at Easter (BELLI'S NOTE).

p. 55, *church-shy folk… ticket broker*: In this period it was obligatory for people to take communion at Easter, and those who did received a ticket from their priest to prove that they had done so. The sextons ran a black market in these tickets, so that the more reluctant churchgoer could simply buy a ticket and thus avoid going to church.

p. 58, *pasqualino*: See the two notes above.

p. 58, *Serpenti*: An area in the Monti district (BELLI'S NOTE).

p. 62, *Repisscitto*: *Repiscitto*, or *ripiscitto*, is the usual nickname given to peasants (BELLI'S NOTE).

p. 65, *An Audience… Scotsmen*: In April 1834 the Pope received two clan chieftains from Scotland who were wearing full Highland attire.

p. 67, *you're taken… tricks*: "You're taken with your genitals"; according to Christian tradition, at the Day of Judgement all the souls that have ever lived are reunited with their bodies. See Belli's sonnet 'Judgement Day' on p. 9.

p. 67, *Vicar General*: The Cardinal Vicar, or Vicar General, is an auxiliary of the Pope and is in charge of the day-to-day management of the diocese of Rome; presumably the narrator sees him as the most appropriate official to be concerned with the management of people even after death.

p. 70, *chincajjere*: The bric-a-brac shop owner Francescangeli devised a way of getting rid of his unsold stock by creating a lottery and attaching a number to each of the 8,193 "prizes", which were then randomly drawn (BELLI'S NOTE).

p. 71, *Palace Teodoli*: Palazzo Teodoli – the accent is on the "o", Te-*o*-do-li – is a Renaissance building on the Via del Corso. It was not unusual for such buildings to have shops to rent on the ground floor and in the courtyard, in one of which the action of this poem no doubt takes place.

p. 75, *Gordon knots… Sollymom*: The narrator is mangling the terms "Gordian knots" and "Solomon".

p. 77, *The Unrepentant*: From an annotation by Belli, the inspiration for this poem is clear: "In 1834 a lower-class man killed an aristocrat who had deflowered his daughter. The man was condemned to death, and didn't want to listen to the priests, the sacraments, etc."

p. 77, *the Bridge*: The bridge in question is Ponte Sant'Angelo, which was one of the places in Rome where executions were conducted.

p. 81, *Casamia*: A *Casamia* was a popular almanac used to foresee the future (and to predict winning Lotto numbers); the almanac was named after Pietro G.P. Casamia, a celebrated astronomer, psychic and cabalist. By citing this figure, Belli is making it plain that he feels the priest giving the sermon is little better than a charlatan.

p. 82, *Tordinone*: The royal theatre in Rome (BELLI'S NOTE).

p. 87, *the prefect of the Sacristry... authentications*: The prefect of the Papal Sacristry had the care of all the relics (and their proofs) collected down the ages by various Popes.

p. 87, *Christ's foreskin... pride and joy*: Belli is perhaps being a little harsh in his satire on the Church's interest in relics, in that this particular relic was never actually claimed to be in the care of the Papacy.

p. 91, *The King of France*: King Louis-Philippe (1773–1850).

p. 91, *Booliyard doo Temply*: Boulevard du Temple in Paris.

p. 91, *Monsure Jack Gerard*: Monsieur Jacques Gérard; this was the false name originally given by the assassin, Joseph Fieschi (1790–1836) from Corsica. Fieschi carried out his attack in July 1835. He was executed the following year.

p. 91, *a load of people... meant*: Eighteen people were killed.

p. 91, *and yet the King... missed*: In fact the King was very lightly injured.

p. 93, *Madame Letizia*: Maria Letizia Bonaparte, the mother of Napoleon, lived in Rome for many years and died there in February 1836, aged eighty-five, some five months after Belli wrote this sonnet.

p. 101, *a mallow pot*: Used for making mallow water, a type of herbal drink with medicinal properties.

p. 101, *I'll drop them... little basket*: Lowering and raising baskets between the street and a tenement window, or between two different tenement windows, was a very common way of moving goods in Rome.

Index of Titles and First Lines

Extra Material

on

Belli's *Sonnets*

Belli's Life

Giuseppe Gioacchino Belli (the middle name is also *Birth and Background* spelt Gioachino) was born on 7th September 1791 in the Sant'Eustachio district in Rome, in a house probably located between Piazza Navona and the Pantheon. His father Gaudenzio had married Luigia Mazio in July 1790, and three more children followed Giuseppe's birth: Carlo in 1792, Flaminia in 1801 and Antonio in 1802. Giuseppe's ancestors were originally from the Marche region, north-east of Rome, then part of the Papal States. One of these ancestors migrated to Rome in the 17th century; his grandson Lorenzo became first the coachman and then the stable master of the illustrious Chigi family, while Lorenzo's son Antonio – Giuseppe's grandfather – effected a move up the social ladder by becoming a bookkeeper for the Rospigliosi family. Bookkeeping was a profession subsequently followed by Belli's father Gaudenzio and others in his family, including the poet himself. Gaudenzio cemented the Bellis' upwards social mobility with business dealings, employment in public offices and an advantageous marriage to Luigia, who came from a family of Neapolitan bankers. By the time of Giuseppe's birth, Gaudenzio and Luigia Belli's purchase on a middle-class lifestyle was as firm as the precarious times allowed – which wasn't firm enough, as subsequent events were to prove.

Something of the nature of Belli's early childhood with his parents can be found in an autobiographical letter titled *My Life* – probably intended for his friend Filippo Ricci – that he wrote at the age of twenty. Whereas his mother loved gaiety and social pleasures, his father was excessively severe: "Never did I see him smile at me, rarely was he pleased with me, and he was forever solicitous to hurt my sensitive pride." In later

139

years Belli appreciated that his father's severity was well-meaning and intended to teach him honesty – he even blesses his father for it in his letter. But it is no wonder that some of the mortifications he endured stayed with him for years. One such incident – when Giuseppe was only seven years old – involved his being accused of stealing a coin from his father's desk. His punishment was to be shut up in a dark room for two days with only bread and water to eat. For a child of his acute sensibility, probably even harder to bear than the physical and emotional deprivation of such a punishment was the ensuing psychological torment: on the third day, Giuseppe was hauled out of his prison and presented before some kind of Grand Inquisition, where "in the presence of about twenty relations I heard myself accused of theft by my father".

Upheavals in Fortune   The poet's childhood was almost as prone to upheaval as Europe herself. The end of the eighteenth century was an intensely volatile period in many parts of the Continent. The French revolution had sent violent shockwaves across other countries, as exemplified by the French-backed Roman Republic taking control of Rome in February 1798. Political power was wrested from the Papal State, and Pope Pius VI was sent into exile, where he died. Much to the dismay of Gaudenzio Belli, a conservative papal loyalist, the jacobins were now in charge. In November 1798, the Neapolitan Gennaro Valentini – a relative of the Bellis, and a general in the Bourbon army opposing the French – entered Rome secretly to try and organize a plot against the jacobins. Staying with Gaudenzio and Maria, and with reinforcements from Naples, he helped lead a counter-revolution and succeeded in forcing the French out of the city. But it was a short-lived success, and the republican forces re-established control by 15th December. Valentini tried to flee, but was captured by the French and excecuted, by firing squad, on 28th December. The Belli family was now in danger of reprisals and retribution, and it was decided that Maria and the children should seek safety in the Kingdom of Naples. The journey was dangerous and traumatic – they were robbed of all their luggage and valuables en route – and the refuge they found in Naples with an uncle was by no means secure, since Maria was suspected by some of having betrayed Valentini. Meanwhile, in Rome, the authorities punished the Belli family by consficating all their possessions.

The Roman Republic was not a success, collapsing by June 1800. With the political authority of the Church re-established, Gaudenzio Belli and his young family were restored into an even more favourable position than they had been in before the Republic. Gaudenzio, in reward for his loyalty to the Papal State, and in compensation for the harm he had suffered, was offered by Pope Pius VII a lucrative position in the port of Civitavecchia, about fifty miles west of Rome. But if the Bellis were now once more materially and politically secure, young Giuseppe's psychological stability was still precarious. Although Gaudenzio's profitable business speculations contributed to the household becoming a much more sociable place than before, Giuseppe's description of the situation is less than flattering to his parents: "My father had become the idol of parasites, and my mother – beautiful as she was – the object of praise and romantic adulation. I, meanwhile, though still a child, strongly condemned their conduct in my heart..."

The swings of fortune in Giuseppe's early life continued *Further Hardships* when, in 1802, an outbreak of cholera occurred in Civitavecchia. As Gaudenzio tried to provide help to the population, he contracted the disease himself, dying on 25th March. The household was now without a secure income, and Maria Belli – who according to her son possessed "an exquisite skill in every kind of feminine work" – turned to needlework to support her children. The family moved from the luxury of their life in Civitavecchia back to Rome, to a modest second-floor apartment at number 391 Via del Corso. Perhaps mercifully, Giuseppe's brother Antonio, who was born later that year, died soon after his birth. The Bellis remained in their Via del Corso apartment until 1807, enduring the daily struggle to keep up with respectability under the constraints of genteel poverty. As Belli later wrote, "No more travels, no more hopes, no more reason for joy..." But although circumstances were much reduced, Maria Belli and her children were not utterly impoverished, and Giuseppe – "already given to literature and reflection, and possessed of a tenacious will to succeed" – was benefiting from the kind of wide, intensive education that his intelligence and ambition craved. Studying at the Collegio Romano, he was interested in all subjects – Latin, rhetoric, poetics, philosophy and science. His curiosity was eclectic, as proven when, later in life, he started to compile his *Zibaldone,* an enormous compendium of articles on all manner of topics. But literature was Giuseppe's greatest passion, and he wrote his first sonnet (in literary Italian, not in the Romanesco dialect that he would later excel in) at the age of fourteen. It is a poem he would annotate many years afterwards with the words "porcheria buggiarona" ("utter crap"). Nevertheless, it marks the beginning of his apprenticeship as a poet, which produced – over the course of the next ten years – at least seventy-two Italian sonnets and about thirty other conventional compositions.

In order to secure a reliable future for her family, Luigia had remarried in 1806 to Michele Mitterpoch, a theatrical agent turned stockbroker who lived in the same neighbourhood. But their marriage was short-lived. As Giuseppe later wrote: "My mother was ill for some time from a long and painful disease, produced without a doubt by the deep afflictions lying heavily on her heart." On 5th October 1807, after five months of illness, and apparently impressing upon her sixteen-year-old son "the obligations of a Christian, a subject and a citizen", Luigia died, at the age of thirty-five.

On her death, the children were taken in by Gaudenzio's brother Vincenzo, who lived in nearby Piazza Lucina, but the arrangement was a miserable one for all concerned, because of the jealousy of Vincenzo's wife, who made them feel unwelcome and forced them to move into the home of Gaudenzio's sister Maddalena, a widow living on the other side of Piazza Navona, at number 2 Via della Fossa. Being shunted around reluctant relatives for support was a grave humiliation for Giuseppe, with his acute sense of pride and dignity. But escaping that charity didn't seem to lessen his sense of grievance: "Resentment at having to feed us quickly led our relatives to procure bookkeeping jobs for my brother and me, so that we could earn our keep". This arrangement meant that the deeply studious boy was no longer able to pursue a formal education. From this point in his life, Belli was to be an autodidact.

Independence   By his own admission, Belli's natural disposition was reserved and somewhat melancholic, but according to his 1811 retrospective letter *My Life* he went through a dissolute stage, giving himself up "to the religion of the senses". The death of his mother, the cessation of his formal studies, the necessity of work, the humiliation of home life and a small amount of disposable income in his pocket led him to the distractions of billiards, ball games and other sports, parties, dinners, late-night entertainment, mock speeches and "knocking around mostly with loose women". Perhaps he had more time to engage in such activites after 1809, when political instability in Rome led to Belli and many other employees with short service being laid off on a small pension.

During these years, Giuseppe was labouring hard on poetry and cultural studies, writing Italian poetry in numerous forms – including much sacred verse, despite his perhaps rather self-conscious and not wholly convincing surrender to the dissolute – mastering French and writing in it, and studying English.

In 1811 Giuseppe found relief from his invidious home life by going to live with the family of his friend Filippo Ricci. Later that year he became the secretary to Prince Stanisław Poniatowski, the nephew of the last king of Poland. In this year he also signalled his writing pretensions by joining a literary club, l'Accademia degli Elleni, founded in 1809 by the archaelogist and art historian Antonio Nibby. By now his literary output was committed and various: Italian lyric poetry in many stanza forms (including sonnets), translations, religious verses and his first published work, in prose: *The Pestilence in Florence in the Year of Our Lord 1348*.

After just one year of employment, following some clashes with Prince Stanisław's wife Caterina, Belli was suddenly dismissed. At first he was helped by the abbot Michele Viale-Prelà, then he found refuge at a cappuccini monastery in Piazza Barberini; in the end he was assisted by Father Ludovico Micara, later a Cardinal, who found him a job as a copyist transcribing the unpublished works of the fifteenth-century writer Bernardino Baldi. To make ends meet he also gave private lessons in Italian, Geography and Mathematics.

The extent of Belli's immersion in literature and culture during his early twenties can be seen in his involvement as one of the founder members in a new literary association, the Accademia Tiberina. A splinter group of the francophile Accademia degli Elleni, the academy's main interest lay in promoting historical studies about Rome. Other key founders were Belli's friends Francesco Spada, Domenico Biagini and Giacomo Ferretti (the famous librettist), and well-known intellectuals and liberals such as Mauro Cappellari, who would later become Pope Gregory XVI. In 1814 a booklet was commissioned to mark the society's first year of existence, which gathered together all the compositions recited during the meetings, including Belli's first published poetry, a sonnet called 'The Toilette'.

Family Life   On 12th September 1816 the twenty-five-year-old Belli married Maria Conti. She had been widowed in January of the same year, though she had been separated from her demented husband, Count Giulio Pichi, since 1813. Maria was ten years older than Giuseppe, and independently wealthy. The alliance was another of those changes in financial security – precipitous drops and sudden upturns – to which Belli seemed peculiarly prone for much of his life, and it provided him with ample security and time to commit himself to literature. If the marriage was not one of intense passion, it was at least characterized by deep respect and affection. The couple took over the second floor of one of Maria's properties, Palazzo Poli. Occupying sixteen rooms and being attended to by liveried servants amongst precious furniture and artefacts was an innovation that Belli adapted to fairly easily. Perhaps out of pride, however, he also took intermittent employment with the Registry Office. Later in life he regretted not making a brilliant civil career, but his many leaves of absence for travelling, his short length of service and his desultory commitment suggest that this regret was mainly wishful thinking.

In 1817 Giuseppe and Maria had their first child, Felice Maria, who died only two years later. In contrast to his own father, Belli is known to have been an unusually caring and attentive parent, so we can infer that his daughter's death was a very heavy blow for him. His only other child, Ciro, born in 1824, became the centre of his life. When Ciro was sent to boarding school in Perugia, Belli travelled there frequently in order to be near him – in 1833 he spent four months there, while the year after that he stayed there three times. The father also wrote reams of caring and solicitous letters to his son when he couldn't be with him. He involved himself intimately in his son's life throughout Ciro's childhood and beyond, to a degree that would be notable even now, but was particularly unusual for its time.

Belli's life as a married man comprised family affairs, literary pursuits, writing letters, maintaining friendships, travelling extensively throughout Italy in connection with his wife's properties and compiling – from 1823 – the *Zibaldone*, a collection of articles and notes on all manner of artistic and scientific topics, manifesting the width and depth of Belli's cultural interests. This endeavour grew over many years until its 4,525 numbered entries and numerous unnumbered ones filled eleven large volumes. Typical entries are anecdotes, bibliographic items, news stories, articles about geography, history, science and religion, and above all there are summaries of the books he read and transcriptions of extracts – intended for himself and for his son Ciro later in life – as well as numerous notes and annotations, including many Romanesco expressions that he had heard on the streets of Rome.

1817 was also the year of Belli's first recorded Romanesco poem, 'Sora Ninetta', a piece of occasional verse in octaves. But Belli remained firmly wedded to the Italian language for many more years: of the pieces that are known about from 1817 to 1829, Italian verse outnumbers Romanesco verse by fifteen to one. Belli's Italian poems were published throughout his life in various formats, including journals and, later, in books, but without ever attracting the critical attention or the recognition the poet was hoping for.

Belli's travels, beginning with a voyage to Venice and Ferrara, were ostensibly concerned with his wife's financial interests, which were connected to land and property. However, he would often go away for weeks or even months on end, often to stay near his son or to visit close personal and literary friends. This was particularly the case after he became acquainted in 1821 with the lively and cultured twenty-one-year-old Vincenza Roberti, the daughter of a marquis, often referred to as "Cencia" by the poet. They would remain friends for over thirty years, their platonic relationship inspiring many romantic verses – fifty sonnets and many songs in 1822 alone – and a hefty correspondence.

Later during his married life Belli found another young object of chaste adoration. The one Romanesco sonnet published in Belli's lifetime with the poet's consent was 'Er padre e la fijja', written in 1835 in connection with a play that was featuring Amalia Bettini, whom he had become acquainted with in September. Bettini was a celebrated actress of her time and a woman of learning; a mutual admiration developed

145

between the two of them, as is evinced by their copious correspondence. When Bettini left Rome in 1836, she bore with her an autograph book of Italian and Romanesco prose and poetry composed by Belli. His affection for Bettini wasn't only romantic: he had a genuine passion for the theatre, and indeed reviewed many dramas for the cultural journal *Lo Spigolatore*, run by his friend Ferretti. His interest in theatre seemed to generate a renewed interest in Italian poetry in the years 1834–35, when he wrote many poems about actresses and singers for Ferretti's journal.

Milan and Carlo Porta   If marriage to Maria Conti represented a structural revolution in Belli's domestic and financial security, it was his journey to Milan in July 1827, and the discovery of Carlo Porta's (1775–1821) Milanese-dialect poetry, that triggered the great literary revolution of his life. He kept a journal of his voyage, partly in French – the *Journal du Voyage de 1827* – and on 22nd August he wrote: "Got up at eight, got ready, read the Milanese poems of the late Carlo Porta". Early the next month, he continued reading Porta's poems from a copy belonging to his host, and on 7th September he bought an edition of the poems for himself. As well as an unfinished rendering of Dante's *Divine Comedy* into dialect, Porta's dialect poetry includes portraits of vivid Milanese characters, attacks on religious hypocrisy and superstition, and political satires – often using the sonnet form.

On his return to Rome, Belli resigned "for ever" from the Accademia Tiberina, the literary society he had helped to found. Whether conscious or unconscious, this act can be seen as deeply symbolic, distancing him – at least for some time – from the decorous literary language and preoccupations of Italian poetry in which he and his contemporaries were involved, in preparation for the vernacular output of Romanesco poetry that was to come three years later. His flow of original creative work almost dried up as he effected a change in mindset. During this time he engaged in a close reading of Porta, as revealed by his annotated copy of the poems, with many Romanesco parallels to obscure Milanese terms flagged up within the margins. Belli must have had a lot of time to pursue this interest: in 1828 he gave up his desultory commitment to working at the Registry Office, somehow wangling another small pension along the way.

The poet visited Milan again in 1828 and a third time in

1829. The way he writes about these visits shows that he was not just thinking about Porta and Milan and Milanese, but about himself and Rome and Romanesco. In 1828 he wrote his first Romanesco sonnet that wasn't a piece of occasional verse, and in 1829 he wrote a further two Romanesco sonnets. At first sight it would seem that his new apprenticeship was completed by 1830, when he composed a seemingly healthy eighty-one Romanesco sonnets; but the real outpouring was to commence the following year.

A remarkable 216 Romanesco sonnets in the year 1831 were followed by a scarcely credible 391 Romanesco sonnets in 1832... Between 1831 and 1837, Belli composed a staggering 1,950 Romanesco sonnets, ninety per cent of which were written in the first five years. Belli was now in his early forties, and in his poetic prime. Steeped in an immense amount of reading and prosodic craft, free of financial worries and work, domestically secure, marinaded in a lifetime's exposure to the infuriating squalor and splendour that was nineteenth-century Rome, and employing the licence of dialect to access the kind of subject matter and language that no other poets in Europe were dealing in, he threw himself heart and soul into his new creative project.

The Romanesco Explosion

In his earliest tranche of poems Belli is often finding his way, with many of the poems being versions of Porta's Milanese sonnets. However, even at the beginning of the journey he created some of his finest poems, in particular 'Er ricordo' ('The Recollection'), 'Er giorno der giudizzio' ('Judgement Day'), 'La fin der monno' ('The End of the World') and 'Er mortorio de Leone Duodescimosiconno' ('The Funeral of Pope Leo XII'). Other remarkable poems from his 1831–37 period include 'Chi vva la notte, va a la morte' ('Who Travels by Night Is a Dead Man'), 'Li soprani der monno vecchio' ('The Bosses of the Old World'), 'La vita dell'omo' ('The Life of Man'), 'Er caffettiere fisolofo', ('The Philosophic Café Proprietor'), 'La risurrezzion de la carne' ('The Resurrection of the Flesh'), 'L'Inferno' ('Hell'), 'Li du' ggener'umani' ('The Two Kinds of Man'), 'Se more' ('Dying'), 'Li dannati' ('The Damned') and 'La famijja poverella' ('The Poor Family').

As well as writing such poems, in the early 1830s Belli was thinking deeply and seriously about the cultural context and relevance of his endeavour. In a letter to Francesco Spada in October 1831 he encloses a "manifesto" for his project – a document he redrafted several times in later years – outlining a grand vision: "I am resolved to leave a monument that shows the common people of Rome as they are today…" At the same time, he was also developing a critical method for his work and trying to work out a system of orthography for the Romanesco dialect.

Belli's extraordinary productivity in Romanesco was already levelling off by 1836, when he produced a comparatively paltry eighty-six sonnets (and seventeen Italian poems). Perhaps this reduction in output was connected to his wife's health; he writes in September about Maria "having for many months lapsed into the same illness again". It is now suspected that she had a brain tumour.

In late June 1837, while staying in Perugia to be near his son Ciro, Belli received a letter about an alarming downturn in Maria's health. By the time he reached Rome, she was dead. He wrote on a picture of her, "Died at midday on Sunday 2nd July, a victim of fatigue and the goodness of her heart." A few months later he wrote to his friend Giuseppe Neroni Cancelli, "What grief! She was everything to me: wife, friend, mother, loving consoler. All of me is dead with her."

Insecurity and the Romanesco Swansong With the death of his wife, the life of ease was over for Belli. He discovered that underneath a smooth surface the family's financial affairs were in a deplorable condition, so much so that he was beseiged by creditors and had to sell off most of the estate. This was the fifth abrupt change in Belli's financial security during his life, only this time he had Ciro to worry about as well. He left behind the expansive luxury of the apartment at Palazzo Poli for a modest dwelling, and applied himself assiduously to building up a secure situation.

The death of his wife also coincided with the death of his passion for his grand Romanesco project, despite a few sporadic flare-ups in later years. Only thirty-three Romanesco poems were written in the five years between 1838 and 1842, while the pull of Italian verse shows itself in the 304 Italian poems he wrote during the same period. Pragmatism was one factor in this change; anxiety about the nature of the public reception of his earthy dialect sonnets – and the effect that a bad reputation would have on his ability to guarantee the future of his son – made itself felt for a few years until he had clawed some security back into his life. This can be seen from a will he wrote in 1837, after an outbreak of cholera in

Rome: "At Mr Domenico Biagini's is a drawer of my verse manuscripts," he writes. "They must be burnt." And despite producing a Romanesco sonnet on 28th September 1838, he writes to Neroni Cancelli a few months later that his poems "must be kept hidden and then burnt, maybe". Perhaps his heart was for them whilst his head was against – after all, he needed a job again.

In 1838 Belli rejoined the society he once claimed to have resigned from "for ever", the Accademia Tiberina, explaining to Ciro in a letter that it was to acquire useful contacts given "the new condition of our household". No longer a gentleman of leisure, he felt unable to express – at least for a time – complete intellectual freedom. At the Accademia Tiberina he found friendship with Monsignor Vincenzo Tizzani (later the Bishop of Terni), who found him employment as the Head of Correspondence at the Ministry of National Debt. He was soon working as a private tutor, too, as in his youth, and by 1840 he was the Secretary of the Academy that he had once renounced. Probably to cement the security of his employment, and to enhance his future prospects, he wrote a plea to Pope Gregory XVI.

In 1841 Ciro returned to Rome from his schooling to study law. Belli followed his progress assiduously, and insisted on supplementing his son's studies with his own teaching, especially in French. Ciro was diligent by nature, and graduated in 1845. His father also took a keen interest in his son's marital prospects, hoping with his old confidante Vincenza Roberti for a union between Ciro and her daughter Matilde – but the two young people, when introduced, did not take to each other.

While his Romanesco poems were mouldering in a drawer under threat of the lick of flames, Belli's Italian poetry was to the fore. Encouraged by his friends Spada, Biagini, Ricci and Tizzani, he published in 1839 *Versi di G.G. Belli Romano,* nearly all the poems within being recent work, while in 1843 he published *Versi inediti*. In 1839 he gave his Romanesco manuscripts to his friend Tizzani – though he took them back again in 1842, demonstrating once more his deep ambivalence to them.

It is thought that as Belli built up his defences against financial insecurity, establishing himself along the way in the friendship and protection of Tizzani, his fears about the possible dangers inherent in his Romanesco poetry were diminishing.

149

And if he had suffered more than a usual number of financial collapses during his life, he was by the same token an unusually fortunate recipient of questionably deserved pensions. Very early in his new employment at the Ministry, one of his major preoccupations was the engineering of favourable conditions for a pension, and he managed to take this pension as soon as January 1845, after his doctor signed him off as unfit for work because of a "general debilitation of the functions of his nervous system". It was his third pension to date, after a career marked by the dilatory commitment to real work of the born writer, and it eased his financial pressures somewhat. By this time, established in the Accademia Tiberina once more, having two volumes of conventional verse under his belt, and enjoying the patronage of Tizzani, he felt free to re-engage with his Roman sonnets.

He would never again approach the outlandish output of 1831–35, but from 1843–45 he added a tidy 127 sonnets to his grand total, including classics such as 'La lavannara zzoppicona' ('The Limping Washerwoman') and 'Er tartajjone arrabbiato' ('The Enraged Stutterer'). In 1846–47 he added a few more, including important pieces such as 'La morte co la coda' ('Death with a Twist') and 'La vita da cane' ('A Dog's Life'); this late flare-up fizzled out in March 1847, and cannot really be said to have revived when, in February 1849, he wrote the last known Romanesco sonnet of his life, 'Sora Crestina Mia' ('My Dear Cristina'), a piece of occasional verse about a terrible cold that afflicted the poet.

In February 1849 the Roman Republic was declared, but the liberals who came into power soon proved to be as venal as the governing authorities they had replaced. Belli was disgusted by them. It seems fitting that his Romanesco sonnets, whose depiction of city life was so dependent on a love-hate relationship with the political, social and religious power of the Papal State, ended in this year.

Last Years   In April 1849, Ciro married Cristina Ferretti, the daughter of Belli's friend Giacomo Ferretti. Belli became extremely close to her. He moved in with his son and daughter-in-law, in an apartment at number 24 Via delle Stimmate. It is likely the wedding was brought forward in an effort to keep Ciro out of the military – the political turbulence of the Roman Republic had resulted in conscription being introduced for young unmarried men, and by all accounts Belli had gone half mad with anxiety that his son would have to go into the army. The political instability affected Belli gravely: perhaps recalling the bloody outcome of another republic in Rome when he was only seven years old, he began to fear once more that his vernacular verse could, one day, prove to be dangerous for him or his son. In any case his thoughts were tending once more towards the incineration of the poems. In a coda to his will this year he instructed Ciro to destroy the vernacular poems after his death "so that they remain unknown to the world, as they are full of reprehensible words, sentences and thoughts". He subsequently moved from words to action, and actually burnt a batch. They are believed to be the drafts and the hand-written copies of his sonnets; but other clean copies – probably in the possession of Tizzani – survived.

Belli was nearing his sixtieth year in 1850, and any liberal sentiments that he may have possessed when younger had long gone, chased on their way by his deep disapproval of the new political order of the republic – a republic that had performed so disastrously as to collapse in chaos after only four months. He became president of the Accademia Tiberina in this year, and wrote passionately against the liberal cause. Once a satirical Romanesco poet, a writer of verses that would have been deemed subversive, obscene and blasphemous by many authorities, he now took on a paid role as a theatrical censor, condemning works by Shakespeare, Verdi and Rossini – among others – during the course of his duties. Over the following years his literary activities became mediocre as he surrendered to the deeply conservative credo from which he had once broken free – theological poetry, liturgical translations.

Always prone to melancholy and depression, gloomy feelings were with him even more in his later years, and he was never able to shake them off. His deep and active attachment to Ciro, Cristina and his grandchildren became his main motivation. When his daughter-in-law died in 1859, after a long illness, aged only thirty-seven, he never really recovered any zest for life himself.

By the end, the poet who had once unleashed a flood of down-to-earth Romanesco poetry – poetry marked by incredible energy and subversive sentiments in every aspect of life, from sex to religion – had dried up to such an extent as to more or less completely renounce not just his Romanesco verse, but the Romanesco language itself. Asked by a senior ecclesiastical friend to translate the Gospel of Mark into the dialect, he refused on the grounds that Romanesco was a corrupt, twisted deviation from the Italian language, suitable only for vulgar expression, not for the reverence of a sacred text.

Belli died of a sudden apoplectic fit on 21st December 1863, some time between eight and nine in the evening. He was buried at the Verano monumental cemetery in Rome.

Belli's Poetry

Background Romanesco is the dialect spoken by the descendants of the original inhabitants of Rome, and it is still very much alive to this day. Though Belli went so far as to renounce his dialect poems in later life, it is abundantly clear that he had set out on his dialect project with a serious and ambitious understanding of its value. Although original and unique in many ways, Belli's vernacular poetry consciously follows a literary tradition inaugurated in Rome more than a century before by such poets as Giovanni Camillo Peresio and Giuseppe Berneri. The putative introduction to a publication that didn't occur within his lifetime expresses Belli's commitment and his perspective: "My purpose is to set down the words of the Roman just as they issue from his mouth, without ornament or alteration, without inversions or poetical licenses..."

The Rome of this era, with its epic religious, social and economic corruption, was an extraordinary society, worthy of the monument Belli erected. It was known as the city of the six Ps – Pope, priests, princes, prostitutes, parasites and the poor – which can hardly be bettered as a concise evocation of the world that Belli's sonnets range over. Conventional nineteenth-century Italian poetry was in no condition to tackle this immense and uncomfortable subject matter, a material so huge and obvious that no other poet saw it. As the Roman novelist Alberto Moravia remarks, "If we think of Belli as the contemporary of the first Romantic generation and the first naturalists, we can assess what an extraordinary phenomenon his poetry is." Amongst the European writers of this era, it was really only the novelists who, as part of their quest to reach great literary heights, were interested in exploring society's ugliest depths. That Belli pulled off this feat of dirty realism in poetry, in the 1830s, is one of the main reasons why his work is very important.

Belli's dominant concern in his Romanesco sonnets is with *Subject Matter* people as they are affected by the place and time and cultual mores in which they live. The poems depict – it seems almost person by person and situation by situation – the life of the people of Rome in the first half of the nineteenth century, and they do so with the technical skill, the range of content, the vernacular wit, the storytelling structure, the quirky eye for detail, the mastery of prosody and the gift for phrase-making that mark a truly memorable poet. Belli gets into the thoughts and problems of every Roman and every reader. We are all there – housewives, mothers, beggars, lovers, business-men, whores, doctors, idiots and optimists; thieves, lawyers, priests, pen-pushers, actresses, depressives, gossips, scientists and waiters; zealots, breast-feeders, stammerers, supplicants, whingers, litigants, sex addicts, wide boys, chancers, chil-dren, soldiers, snobs and liars; a couple of Popes, of course, and oppressors and victims, workers of every ilk, shop girls, servant girls, pregnant girls, chorus girls, yes-men, no-men, con-men, binmen – all men, and all women too. Indeed, Belli is a nineteenth-century poet interested enough in women to try to evoke their often unpleasant experiences rather than a patronizing, idealized version of their gender. The lives of these men and women are generally presented without autho-rial commentary, but often from the jaundiced perspectives of other highly compromised characters. This makes the poems feel distinctly modern, layering them with a complex human-ity and a realism (at times an almost photographic realism, as several commentators have pointed out) that we struggle to find in other poets of the time. When the best of them is con-sidered as a body of work (there is, admittedly, a tranche of bad ones, which is only to be expected when someone writes over 2,000 sonnets), they represent the kind of achievement more usual to the nineteenth-century novel: an entire, credible and incredible, functioning world that the reader dives into gladly and has to be dragged out of reluctantly.

Belli is not known very widely outside Italy, not in the way that his contemporary Leopardi is known, for example – and within Italy itself he is regarded as an important but not a vital figure. Part of the reason is dialect, which is something of a two-edged sword for the poet. On the one hand dialect provides him with the inspiration and the licence to transcend the conventional restrictions of nineteenth-century mores on

153

literary expression (in terms of plain-speaking diction and everyday content he is doing things that Wordsworth and Coleridge in their preface to the *Lyrical Ballads* could hardly have imagined possible); but on the other hand, dialect is undoubtedly the reason for his relative neglect.

Perceptions of Belli's poetry also suffer, perhaps, from perceptions of him. Though clearly a man cherished by many in private life, he was a self-absorbed, unexciting public figure who trimmed his sails to the wind – hardly a brave and principled risk-taker or a social leader. He lived the life of Riley when he could, while mocking the rich in his poetry; and he excoriated the Vatican for its corruption and hypocrisy in his verse while sucking up to it during his life. Alberto Moravia, however, seems almost thankful for the poet's complicity in the wrongs he was satirizing, arguing that it was this dualism at the base of Belli's moral life that underwrites the creative achievement. As Moravia puts it, "only a man like him, deeply timorous and conservative in his soul, could have written these satirical sonnets against the papal government... he could not flee from the deep, guilty but invincible love that the artist has for his subject matter." That is an important and profound point Moravia makes: it is the moral culpability that Belli shares with his targets, his lack of angst in the face of moral contradiction, that endows him with the power to portray the compromised people of Rome and capture their complex humanity. By scrutinizing the human animal full on – often at its lowest, and sometimes at its highest, and best of all at both levels simultaneously – and by rendering so accurately and memorably its frailties, faults and quirks, he gets at our humanity more precisely than do apparently higher-minded poets; and getting at our humanity by making it memorable in aesthetically compelling language is surely one of the greatest functions of poetry.

Form   The sonnet is the most important short lyric form in European poetry, attracting for eight hundred years the talents of most of the great European poets. Belli rates as an important sonneteer because of the quality, artistry, range, content, modernity, realism and memorabilty of his best compositions – and for the sheer quantity of the rest. The satirical sonnet predominates – the condition of Rome in Belli's day provided almost infinite subject matter in this regard – but a careful look at his work shows that there are many modes and moods in his exploitation of the sonnet form. As well as the hundreds of everyday characters and situations presented by Belli satirically, a significant proportion of his sonnets eschew satire for pathos, empathy, lyricism and quirkiness. There are also Biblical retellings, sonnets about legends and history, and quasi-experimental linguistic riffs. We could think of his Romanesco oeuvre as something akin to a *Canterbury Tales* or a *Decameron* of sonnets. The lyrical beauty and sadness of 'Li malincontri' ('A Terrible Encounter'), the wonderful maternal ambiguities of 'Le smammate' ('Coochy-coochy-coo'), the delightful minor-key quirkiness of 'Li connimenti' ('The Ingredients'), the extreme conversational realism of 'Le dimanne a ttesta per aria' ('This and That'), the brutal fatalism of 'La vita dell'omo' ('The Life of Man'), the social observation of 'Li gatti dell'appiggionante' ('The Tenant's Cats'), demonstrate that a sonneteer need not be a one-trick pony. The apparent barriers imposed on language by "restrictive" poetic form are actually one of the gateways through which the deepest levels of literary achievement can find release. In Belli's endlessly inventive treatment of the sonnet, this glorious paradox is exemplified.

Only one of Belli's Romanesco sonnets was published during his lifetime with his consent, 'Er padre e la fijja', which appeared in a theatre publication in 1835. But some of the poems were circulated amongst friends in manuscript form and in letters, and were recited at gatherings by Belli himself (finding such early admirers as Gogol and Saint-Beuve); inevitably some leaked out into the general public domain and – in an age without clear copyright laws – were published without consent. For nearly thirty years it was just the occasional poem or two cropping up here and there, with 'La vita da cane' in particular making regular appearances, but in 1862 a book titled *Il poeta travesterino: raccolta di poesie giocose in romanesco* (*The Poet of Travestere: A Collection of Humorous Poems in Romanesco*) lifted twenty-two sonnets, while in 1864 two further collections, both entitled *Sonetti umoristici* (*Humorous Sonnets*), printed fifty-one and three respectively.

Publication History of Belli's Romanesco Sonnets

Belli's son and friends – even his ecclesiatical friends such as Cardinal Tizzani – recognized the worth of his Romanesco sonnets and, far from trying to destroy them or surpress them as ambiguously requested, arranged for a selection of them to be published after Belli's death; perhaps even they would

155

have been surprised to know, however, that Belli's Romanesco work would gain a far higher reputation than his poetry in Italian. Between 1865–66 they published the four-volume *Poesie inedite di Giuseppe Gioachino Belli* (*Unpublished Poems by Giuseppe Gioachino Belli*). Each volume had two parts, the first devoted to poetry in Italian in various forms, and the second to sonnets in Romanesco. The four volumes contained 797 sonnets in total, with a text largely bowdlerized by the editors.

Poesie inedite di Giuseppe Gioachino Belli was used by other publishers, and in 1869 a publication called *Sonetti satirici in dialetto romanesco attribuiti a G.G.B.* (*Satirical Sonnets in the Romanesco Dialect attributed to G.G.B.*) appeared, followed in 1870 by *Duecento sonetti in dialetto romanesco di G.G.B.* (*Two Hundred Sonnets in Romanesco Dialect by G.G.B*). These two publications helped in diffusing Belli's Romanesco work.

The first collected and scholarly edition, edited by Luigi Morandi, was produced in six volumes between 1886–89. It contains copious ancillary material, including a 64-page concordance of the proper names within the sonnets, a 54-page glossary and a 150-page preface. The first five volumes present the sonnets in chronological order, except for the most sensitive poems, which are gathered in the sixth volume, together with the thirty-four-sonnet sequence 'Er còllera mòribbus' and some apocryphal Italian and Romanesco sonnets.

The first modern, scholarly complete edition was edited by Giorgio Vigolo and published in 1952. It contains all 2,279 poems, and employs a uniform orthography. Several other complete editions have been published since then, including the definitive ten-volume *Poesie romanesche* (1988–93) edited by Roberto Vighi and the 1998 two-volume edition *Tutti i sonetti romaneschi* edited by Marcello Teodonio, which has an introduction, chronology of life and works, and extensive bibliographies on all aspects of Belli and Belli scholarship.

English and Scots Translations

Belli was first introduced to English language speakers by the journal *The Fortnightly Review* in 1874, in an article by Hans Sotheby, who glosses eleven sonnets and provides an acute appraisal of the poetry and the dialect. In 1881 Frances Eleanor Trollope and her husband Thomas Adolphus Trollope (brother of the novelist Anthony Trollope) brought out a publication called *The Homes and Haunts of the Italian Poets*; Eleanor Trollope's introduction to Belli in this book was first published in *Belgravia* a year earlier. Trollope – like Sotheby before her – comments on the extreme realism of Belli's work. She provides translations of nine poems, and she is the first translator to render Belli into metrical and rhyming English, something she does exceedingly well in at least a couple of her translations.

Modern interest in Belli in English translation begins with Eleanor Clark, who published an essay on Belli in her 1953 book *Rome and a Villa*. Clark was a commentator and novelist rather than a poet and translator, but her eleven prose translations and her modern exploration of Belli's place in Italian literature – his themes, technique, use of dialect – set the scene for the first modern translators. These are Harold Norse, Anthony Burgess, Miller Williams and Allen Andrews.

Belli in Twentieth-century English Translations

The first book of translations into English was *The Roman Sonnets of Giuseppe Gioachino Belli*, by the American poet Harold Norse (*b*.1916), a writer linked with the Beat Generation, and an associate of writers such as William Carlos Williams, William Burroughs, Allen Ginsberg, Gregory Corso, W.H. Auden, Christopher Isherwood, Lawrence Ferlinghetti and Charles Bukowski. It was published in 1960 and contained forty-six translations, with a foreword by William Carlos Williams, a thoughtful note on translating Belli from Norse himself and, in a later edition, an informative essay on Belli by Alberto Moravia. The book provided a valuable introduction to Belli's content and themes for non-Italian speakers, and Norse clearly identified with the hand-to-mouth lives and street language of many of the characters in Belli's poems. His lines shy away from any kind of metrical measure or syllabic count, and deal in rhyme and slant rhyme intermittently. He sometimes applies an argot of New Yorkese to render the vernacular.

Harold Norse

In 1977 the English novelist Anthony Burgess (1917–93) published his novel *ABBA ABBA* – the title is derived from the rhyme scheme of the octet in a Petrarchan sonnet. The story is set around the last months in the life of the great English Romantic poet John Keats, who died of tuberculosis in Rome

Anthony Burgess

157

in 1821, and explores the possibility that Keats and Belli became acquainted with one another. At the back of the novel is an appendix containing seventy-one translations by Burgess of Belli's sonnets. Some of these translations are pitched in a Manchester dialect. In keeping with the novel, the pretence is maintained that these translations were composed by one Joseph Joachim Wilson, an English descendent of one of the book's characters. All of the translations are derived from Belli's biblical sonnets – exemplified in the present volume by 'Er giorno der giudizzio' ('Judgement Day'), 'La scirconcisione der Zignore' ('The Circumcision of the Lord') and 'Un zentimento mio' ('My Opinion') – which makes Burgess's contribution a very idiosyncratic one.

Of the four translators of Belli into English under discussion, Burgess is easily the most ambitious from a poetical point of view. His poems are vigorous and earthy and linguistically memorable, are written in iambic pentameter, and pay full adherence to the strict rhyme scheme of a Petrarchan sonnet; this last aspect of his translations is a very difficult objective when translating from rhyme-rich Romanesco into rhyme-meagre English, and one that requires superlative prosodic gifts if it is to be executed well. In Burgess's case, the costs it incurs in other areas of the great balancing act of translating formal verse in one language into formal verse of another can be noticeable. In particular, he can digress from Belli's content so extensively at times as to make for versions that are only lightly related to the originals; and in other cases, he uses the kind of contortions, abbreviations and syntactical compression that more skilful practioners of formal verse – such as the Scots translators Robert Garioch and William Neill, for example – wouldn't countenance. But not to be lightly dismissed is the fact that Burgess's versions are certainly sonnets – something that the other three translators into English cannot reasonably claim. For vigour, voice, a real sense of Belli's spirit and a technical ambition that sometimes pays off and is always interesting even when it fails, Burgess's Belli is well worth reading.

Miller Williams   The 1981 *Sonnets of Giuseppe Belli* is a book of seventy-five translations. Williams, a translator, poet, academic and editor, is also known for reciting a poem at the 1997 inauguration of President Clinton. He includes a helpful introduction to his selection, and a note on the issues involved when translating Belli. This note declares the formal difficulties of translating sonnets and lists the various compromises he has been forced to make because of them; metre and syllable count are abandoned for an accentual-stress count, rhymes are exchanged for slant rhymes. The poems are fairly accurate to the originals, but there is an absence of vigorous voice.

In 1984 a little-known book titled *The People of Rome*   *Allen Andrews*
in 100 Sonnets was published in Italy. Translated by Allen Andrews and presented in parallel Romanesco and English, each poem is beautifully illustrated by Ron Sandford. The translations dip in and out of iambic pentameter, very loose iambic pentameter and no metre at all, and they are unrhymed, which certainly makes them the most free, formally, of all translations so far. However these versions may well appeal to many readers because Allen's language is lively, idiomatic, faithful to the original content, consistent in tone across each poem, and usually natural in expression, with a non-tricksy and plain-speaking authenticity.

It is sometimes asserted – and probably with some merit   *Scots Translations*
– that Scots is better suited to the task of translating the Romanesco language than is English, since the relationship of Romanesco to Italian is said to mirror the relationship of Scots to English: for Romanesco and Scots are not dependent dialects of Italian and English, but sister dialects that lost the battle of becoming the standard language (to Tuscan Italian and South-East English respectively). This makes Romanesco and Scots seem particularly vernacular and lively in general tone to the standard Italian and standard English speaker respectively. Scots verse also enjoys the advantage of being able to employ virtually all available rhymes in English and then a further great tranche of rhymes exclusive to Scots. This advantage has been admirably exploited by two twentieth-century Scots poets, Robert Garioch and William Neill.

The benchmark for any translations of Belli into the domi-   *Robert Garioch*
nant English dialect, or into other English dialects, or into a sister language such as Scots, has to be the work of the Scottish poet Robert Garioch (real name Robert Sutherland, 1909–81). He was an important figure in the literary revival of the Scots language that was spearheaded by Hugh McDiarmid in the mid-twentieth century. Garioch had three great advantages over the translators in English. The first is that he was a first-rate sonneteer before he came to Belli, and

159

so did not need to give up the sonnet's integral metre and rhyme in the quest for a natural diction; the second is one of literary temperament, in that his overriding literary concern is with ordinary people, the "wee man"; and the third is the Scots language itself.

There are 120 translations by Garioch within his posthumously published *Complete Poetical Works* of 1983 – twelve of them are presented in the appendix to this volume. He handles metre and rhyme so skilfully that he creates memorable poetic language without compromising natural expression – a central prosodic ambition and indeed obsession of any great poet in formal verse, and one that Belli himself took very seriously, explaining in his introduction to his Romanesco sonnets that "metre and rhyme must be produced as if by accident, and current words never corrected or manipulated in a way different to what the evidence of the ear suggests". Garioch achieves this even while pulling-off the two-rhyme octet and sextet of the Petrarchan sonnet – something Burgess failed in more often than not. Garioch's vernacular but accessible Scots irresistibly captures the street-based Romanesco language of the originals. His artistic objective is often to transform the sonnets into wholly Scottish versions not just in language but in place and context too, so in that respect his poems are sometimes closer to versions than translations. But the most important aspect of his work is that here are translations whose high formal skill in metre and rhyme makes them authentic sonnets, while his mastery of vernacular expression renders Belli's tone faithfully while (usually) remaining reasonably close to the originals in content. It represents a high achievement in the uncompromising translation of formal verse.

William Neill   The distinguished Scottish poet William Neill (*b*.1922) writes in Scots, English and Gaelic, and his contribution to contemporary poetry, though esteemed, is nevertheless commonly asserted by most commentators to be undervalued. Neill was inspired by Garioch, writing in one of his publications "In memorie o Rab Garioch (Robert Sutherland) whase skeilie owersettin o Belli's *sonetti* first gied me a lift to ettil a hantle mair." Like Garioch, Neill came to Belli as a first-rate sonneteer in his own right, and like Garioch he enjoys the natural advantage of the Scots language. He has published three pamphlets of Belli translations, *A Hantle* o *Romanesco Sonnets*, *Twa Score Romanesco Sonnets* and *Seventeen Sonnets by G.G. Belli*. There is much overlap of content, but in total he has translated forty-one poems. The quality of his Belli translations often matches that of Garioch – if he has received less appreciation for them, the main reason is probably that Garioch got there first.

– Mike Stocks, 2007

Select English Bibliography

English Translations
Andrews, Allen, *The People of Rome in 100 Sonnets* (Rome: Bardi, 1984)
Burgess, Anthony, Appendix to *ABBA ABBA* (London: Faber 1977)
Norse, Harold, *The Roman Sonnets of Giuseppe Gioachino Belli* (Highlands, North Carolina: Jargon, 1960)
Williams, Miller, *Sonnets of Giuseppe Belli* (Baton Rouge, LA: Louisiana State University Press, 1981)

Scots Translations
Garioch, Robert, *Complete Poetical Works*, ed. Robin Fulton (Edinburgh: Macdonald, 1983)
Neill, William, *A Hantle o Romanesco Sonnets bi Giuseppe Gioachino Belli* (Castle Douglas: Burnside Press, 1996)
Neill, William, *Twa Score Romanesco Sonnets bi Giuseppe Gioachino Belli* (Castle Douglas: Burnside Press, 1996)
Neill, William, *Seventeen Sonnets by G.G. Belli*, (Kirkcaldy: Akros, 1998)

Commentary
Clark, Eleanor, *Rome and a Villa* (London: Michael Joseph, 1953)
Garvin, Barbara, 'G.G. Belli and Roman dialect', in *Italian Dialects and Literature From the Renaissance to the Present*, ed. by Emmanuela Tandello and Diego Zancani, Supplement I of the *Journal of the Institute of Romance Studies* (London, 1996), pp. 53-71
Moravia, Alberto, 'Introduction' (in *The Roman Sonnets of Giuseppe Gioachino Belli*, see above)

161

Williams, Miller, 'Introduction' (in *Sonnets of Giuseppe Belli*, see above)
Williams, William Carlos, 'Preface' (in *The Roman Sonnets of Giuseppe Gioachino Belli*, see above)

Select Italian Bibliography

Abeni, Damiano, et al., *Belli oltre frontiera: la fortuna di G.G. Belli nei saggi e nelle versioni di autori stranieri* (Rome: Bonacci, 1983)
Belli, Giuseppe Gioachino, *Sonetti*, ed. Giorgio Vigolo (Milan: Mondadori, *c.*1978)
Belli, Giuseppe Gioachino, *Tutti i sonetti romaneschi*, ed. by Marcello Teodonio, 2 vols. (Milan: Newton & Compton, 1998)
Gibellini, Pietro, *La Bibbia del Belli* (Milan: Adelphi, 1974)
Gibellini, Pietro, *I panni in Tevere: Belli romano e altri romaneschi* (Rome: Bulzoni, 1989)
Merolla, Riccardo, ed., *G.G. Belli romano, italiano ed europeo* (Rome: Bonacci, 1985)
Nappo, Francesco and Sabarini, Raniero, *Belli: epico e popolare* (Rome: Nuova Spada, 1980)
Porta, Carlo, *Poesie*, ed. Dante Isella (Milan: Mondadori, 2000)
Rinaldi, Riccardo, *Giuseppe Gioachino Belli: Vita e antologia di sonetti commentati* (Rome: Nuova Spada, 2002)
Teodonio, Marcello, *Vita di Belli* (Roma: Laterza, 1992)
Vaccaro, Gennaro, *Vocabolario romanesco belliano e italiano-romanesco* (Rome: Romana Libri Alfabeto, 1969)

Appendix

Twelve Translations
by Robert Garioch

Agin The Commies [*Contro li giacobbini*]

Mind whit ye're letting yersel in fir, Jock;
let thaim that bulloxt it redd up the mess:
the warld, dispitous, gaes like a k'nock;
bide ye at hame, mind yer ain fashiousness.

I wadnae bluidy like to be thae folk
that seek the wrack of Rome and Offices;
ye're breengein throu a kyle wi monie a rock,
dunschin yer heid agin the justices.

Mair like the thing, to eat yer breid and spit,
ye ken, nor risk yer thrapple out of greed
to pley the lairdie and growe fat on it.

Let water rin dounbye to the mill-lead;
ye're dear to Gode – I'm shair ye maun admit
hou he's been saving ye yer daily breid.

Mammie's Counsel [*Li conzijji de mamma*]

D'ye see hou folk pit twa and twa thegither
hou thae ear-rings cam intill yer possession?
And you, ye fuil! hae some want, or obsession
wi guilt, or guid kens whit, that garrs ye swither!

Ye neednae tak a tellin frae yer mither,
but jist to profit frae the situation:
if some rich chiel suid mak ye a profession
of sairvice, I'll no garr luve's blossom wither.

Nae dout, this darg has keepit ye gey thrang,
but heize his boat out, set him oarin in it,
and syne he docks the pey: that's an auld sang.

Oh, whan ye hear owre muckle rumour rounit,
be proud; gie him a puckle and think lang.
Wha duisnae save he's sel, my lass, is drounit.

Judgement Day [*Er giorno der giudizzio*]

Fowre muckle angels wi their trumpets, stalkin
til the fowre airts, sall aipen the inspection;
they'll gie a blaw, and bawl, ilk to his section,
in their huge voices: "Come, aa yees, be wauken."

Syne sall crawl furth a ragment, a haill cleckin
of skeletons yerkt out fir resurrection
to tak again their ain human complexion,
like choukies gaitheran roun a hen that's clockan.

And thon hen sall be Gode the blissit Faither;
he'll pairt the indwellars of mirk and licht,
tane doun the cellar, to the ruiff the tither.

Last sall come angels, swarms of them, in flicht,
and, like us gaean to bed without a swither,
they will blaw out the caunnles, and guid-nicht.

The Guid Family [*La bbona famijja*]

Faither wins hame, my grannie leaves her wheel,
puir sowl, gies owre her spinning for the nicht;
she lays the buird, blaws her wee coal alicht,
and we sit-in to sup our puckle kail.

We mak oursels an omelet, aince in a while,
gey thin, sae's ye can fairly see the licht
throu it, jist like it wes a lug: aa richt,
we chaw a puckle nuts, and that's our meal.

While Faither and mysel and Clementine
bide on, she clears the buird, gaes aff and redds
the kitchie, and we drink a drappie wine.

The wee carafe timmit doun till the dregs,
a wee strone, a hailmary said, and syne,
lither and lown, we sclimm intill our beds.

The Weedie wi Sevin Bairns [*La vedova co ssette fijji*]

This month syne I hae sent the youngest wean
til the wee, faur-back Brithers' Schuil, I'm shair
he'll dae aa richt, screives pat-heuks, pretty fair,
and chants the easy nummers by his lane.

Yin's been to Daddie John's a year and mair,
maks umberellies, tither's hewing stane
at St Michael's, the Orphanage has taen
the auldest laddie, they lairn him Latin thair.

Of the three lassies, Nina dee'd, our Annie
is at the Little Clogs' Hospice, and wee
Nunziatina's mindit by her granny.

And I, puir wife, just fend, nae mair, ye see,
darnin thae fowk's duddy socks, I cannae
dae mair, or Our Leddie provides for me.

The Rulers of the Auld Warld [*Li soprani der monno vecchio*]

Yince on a time there wes a King, who sat
screivan this edict in his palace-haa
til aa his fowk: "Vassals, I tell ye flat
that I am I, and you are bugger-aa.

I mak richt wrang, wrang richt, my word is law:
I can sell yese, sae muckle fir the lot:
If I hing yese, ye're no ill-yaised ava,
ye rent yir lives and gear frae me, that's that.

Whasae bides in this warld, bot the title
either of Paip, or Emperor, or King,
sall niver mell in oniething that's vital."

The heidsman tuke this edict roun in sicht
of aa the fowk, speiran anent this thing,
and they aa said til him: *That's richt, that's richt.*

The Condiment of Paradise [*Er companatico der paradiso*]

Eftir Gode had creatit in a week
aa kinna orra things, baith nice and naisty,
in or near Paradise, he made a cleek,
and on thon cleek hingit a ham, gey tasty.

And said, "Thon wife, that niver wes in haste tae
faisten the horns on a man, sall stick
her knife intilt and hae a graund fiesta
wi breid of hevin, hailmeal, our ain bake."

Jist walin them at random, we can say
Eve dee'd, and Leah dee'd, and Abigail
and aa the lave, doun til the present day.

Ilkane of them, knife in her haund, wad fail
to cut a whang, and nane of them cuid hae.
Sax thoosan years, and still thon ham is haill.

The Life of Man [*La vita dell'omo*]

Nine month in the stink, syne rowed-up, dosed wi dill,
mang kisses, milk, greitan and curly locks,
harnessed, happit in babby-clouts and frocks,
in a bairn-fank pentit wi Jack and Jill.

And syne stairs aa the torment of the schuil,
the A.B.C. and chulblains, pawmies, knocks,
the cackie doun the hole, a puckle poax,
rush-fever, measles or some ither ill.

Syne lairnin hou to fast and mak a levin,
the rent, the government, the presoun cell,
hospital, dyvourie, mockage and grieving,

the simmer suin, the winter snaw and haill…
And at the feenish o't, Gode bliss us, even
eftir aa thon, comes daith and, lastly, hell.

The Philosopher Café Proprietor [*Er caffettiere fisolofo*]

Men in this warld, whan aa's said and duin,
are juist like coffee beans in a machne:
first yin, anither, and ae mair, they rin
til the same destiny, that's easy seen.

They keep aye cheengin places, a big yin
shouthers its wey afore a smaller bean;
they croud the entrance, fechtan their wey in,
syne the mill grinds them doun and throu the screen.

Sae in this warld ilka man maun boun
intill fate's neive, thair to be passed and passed
frae haun til haun and birlit roun and roun;

and aa thae folk, aye muvan slaw or fast,
maun gang, unkennan, til the boddum doun,
and faa intill daith's thrapple at the last.

The Astrologer [*Lo stroligo*]

Jist walk doun onie street ye like to try,
whaur there's a hole in the grund, ye'll see gey few
of aa the fowk that happen to gae by
that dinnae hae a keek doun at the view.

Is tap-soil different frae soil doun-bye?
Whit are they curious to see, that's new?
Whit can it be, they're aa sae keen to spy?
That they may find Beelzebub's burroo?

Whit's waur, I cannae mak out why they stare
doun in this hole in the grund, wi blearit ee,
whaur there is nut wan bluidy thing doun thair.

That maks the warld dafter, aa the same,
nor I am, seeing frae my balcony
sterns in the luift, and whit there is in thaim.

The Puir Family [*La famijja poverella*]

Wheesht nou, my darling bairnies, bide ye quaet:
yir faither's comin suin, jist bide a wee.
Oh Virgin of the greitin, please help me,
Virgin of waymenting, ye that can dae't.

My hairts, I wuss that ye cuid ken hou great
my luve is! Dinnae greit, or I sall dee.
He'll bring us something hame wi him, you'll see,
and we will get some breid, and ye will eat…

Whit's that ye're sayin, Joe? jist a wee while,
my son, ye dinnae like the dark ava.
Whit can I dae fir ye, if there's nae yle?

Puir Lalla, whit's the maitter? Oh my bairn,
ye're cauld? But dinnae staund agin the waa:
come and I'll warm ye on yir mammie's airm.

I Hae Witnesses [*E cciò li tistimònî*]

Whan yesterday I saw the Halie Faither
gae frae the Nunziata by Pasquin's Square,
ye shuid hae seen his face, he gied a glare
like a Guairds corporal under the weather.

As he rade past, he had a rare auld blether
wi Cardinal Orioli and Ffarcoggner'
sitting forenenst him, a gey mim-moued pair,
side-for-side, wheesht-wheesht, speechless aathegither.

The crowd wes cheering meantime and applauding,
and he quick benedictionation spraying
baith sides the coach, like pour-outs at a waddin.

Syne wi his muckle haunds he gaed on laying
doun the law to thon pair, their heids nid-nodding;
they gree'd wi him, whitever he wes saying.

Acknowledgements

Many people have contributed to the writing and publication of this book. I am grateful to Professor Steve Ellis at the University of Birmingham for providing encouraging feedback and for pointing out a path to publisher, to Matteo Bonotti for helping me to choose a shortlist of poems to translate, and to Professor Giuseppe Di Palma at the University of Berkeley for generously giving up time to check and amend many of my preparatory literal prose translations of Belli's poems. Paul Howard of Oxford University graciously let me read his unpublished article 'A Study of a Selection of G.G. Belli's Sonnets and their Existing Translations', and has allowed me to utilize in the Extra Material the information he has assembled on awareness of Belli in nineteenth-century Britain. I and Oneworld Classics are indebted to Dr Ennio Troili at the Italian Cultural Institute in Edinburgh, who secured important funding for the project, and who has been a most gracious support throughout. I am deeply grateful to everyone at Oneworld Classics for all the work they have done on this book, in particular William Chamberlain, Jonny Gallant, Alessandro Gallenzi, Elisabetta Minervini and Christian Müller. Finally and most importantly, I would like to acknowledge my debt and thanks to Alessandro Gallenzi for his close involvement and encouragement at every stage of the book; as a native Romanesco speaker he has been critical in ensuring the translations remain accurate to the originals in content and tone, and as an uncompromising line-by-line aesthetic critic who often said "not good enough yet" he has helped me to make the translations as good as I can get them.

– Mike Stocks, 2007

ONEWORLD CLASSICS

ONEWORLD CLASSICS aims to publish mainstream and lesser-known European classics in an innovative and striking way, while employing the highest editorial and production standards. By way of a unique approach the range offers much more, both visually and textually, than readers have come to expect from contemporary classics publishing.

~

CHARLOTTE BRONTË: *Jane Eyre*

EMILY BRONTË: *Wuthering Heights*

ANTON CHEKHOV: *Sakhalin Island*
Translated by Brian Reeve

CHARLES DICKENS: *Great Expectations*

D.H. LAWRENCE: *The First Women in Love*
Unexpurgated Version

JAMES HANLEY: *Boy*

JACK KEROUAC: *Beat Generation*

JANE AUSTEN: *Emma*

WILKIE COLLINS: *The Moonstone*

DESIDERIUS ERASMUS: *Praise of Folly* and
Pope Julius Barred from Heaven
Translated by Roger Clarke

BRAM STOKER: *Dracula*

GIOVANNI BOCCACCIO: *Decameron*
Translated by J.G. Nichols

DANTE ALIGHIERI: *Poems*
Translated by J.G. Nichols

PETRONIUS ARBITER: *Satyricon*
Translated by Andrew Brown

ALEXANDER PUSHKIN: *Eugene Onegin*
Translated by Roger Clarke

FYODOR DOSTOEVSKY: *The Insulted and Injured*
Translated by Ignat Avsey

CONNOISSEUR

The CONNOISSEUR list will bring together unjustly neglected works, making them available again to the English-reading public. All titles are printed on high-quality, wood-free paper and bound in black cloth with gold foil-blocking, end papers, head and tail bands and ribbons. Each title will make a perfect gift for the discerning bibliophile and will combine to make a wonderful and enduring collection.

CECCO ANGIOLIERI: *Sonnets*
Translated by C.H. Scott

BOILEAU: *The Art of Poetry* and *Lutrin*
Translated by William Soames and John Ozell

ANONYMOUS: *The Song of Igor's Campaign*
Translated by Brian Reeve

AMBROSE BIERCE: *The Monk and the Hangman's Daughter*

SAMUEL GARTH: *The Dispensary*

JOHN ARBUTHNOT: *The History of John Bull*

TOBIAS SMOLLETT: *The History and Adventures of an Atom*

ALESSANDRO TASSONI: *The Rape of the Bucket*
Translated by James Atkinson and John Ozell

UGO FOSCOLO: *Poems*
Translated by J.G. Nichols

JOHANN WOLFGANG GOETHE: *Urfaust*
Translated by J.G. Nichols

GIUSEPPE PARINI: *A Fashionable Day*
Translated by Herbert Bower

GIAMBATTISTA VICO: *Autobiography*
Translated by Stephen Parkin

To order any of our titles and for up-to-date information about our
current and forthcoming publications, please visit our website on:

www.oneworldclassics.com